VANESSA PLACE

LAST WORDS

Oui, monsieur, je voudrais demander pardon à la famille de la victime. Il n'y a aucune raison pour expliquer ce que j'ai fait, je ne comprends pas pourquoi je l'ai fait.

Je souhaite que vous puissiez vivre le reste de votre vie sans haine. Je prie le Seigneur, accordez-moi le pardon. Seigneur tout-puissant, je m'en remets à vous, Amen.

Je tiens à signaler que j'ai écrit une déclaration et que le directeur de la prison vous en remettra une copie. Je proclame que je suis innocent, et c'est tout ce que j'ai à dire.

Oui, je veux dire à tous combien je vous aime. Gardez la tête haute. Nous sommes tous de la même famille, le peuple de Dieu Tout-Puissant. Nous sommes tous bons. Je suis prêt.

Sont-ils déjà en train de le faire ? Je vais aller dormir. À plus tard. Ce truc pique, homme tout-puissant.

Je suis un homme innocent. Je n'ai tué personne. Vous allez tuer un innocent. Mon bras gauche me tue. Ça fait très mal.

Au revoir à ma famille ; je vous aime tous, je suis désolé pour la famille de la victime. J'aimerais pouvoir obtenir leur pardon.

Je veux que ceux-là, là-bas, continuent de lutter contre la peine de mort. Oui, je le veux. Monsieur, en l'honneur d'un véritable héros américain. « Et que ça roule ! »

Seuls le ciel et l'herbe verte sont éternels et aujourd'hui est un bon jour pour mourir.

Je n'ai pas de dernière déclaration. Je suis prêt.

Ce condamné a refusé de faire une dernière déclaration.

Yes sir, I would like to ask forgiveness of the family. I have no reason for why I did it, I don't understand why I did it.

I hope that you can live the rest of your lives without hate. I pray the Lord grant me forgiveness. All powerful and almighty Lord I commit myself to thee, Amen.

I would like to point out that I have written a statement and the Warden will give you a copy. I still proclaim I am innocent, and that's all I have to say.

Yes, I want to tell everybody that I love everybody. Keep your heads up. We are all family, people of God Almighty. We're all good. I'm ready.

Are they already doing it? I'm gonna go to sleep. See you later. This stuff stings, man almighty.

I'm an innocent man. I did not kill anyone. Ya'll are killing an innocent man. My left arm is killing me. It hurts bad.

Goodbye to my family; I love all of you, I'm sorry for the victim's family. I wish I could make it up to them.

I want those out there to keep fighting the death penalty.

Yes I do. Sir, in honor of a true American hero. "Let's roll".

Only the sky and the green grass goes on forever and today is a good day to die.

I have no last words. I am ready.

This offender declined to make a last statement.

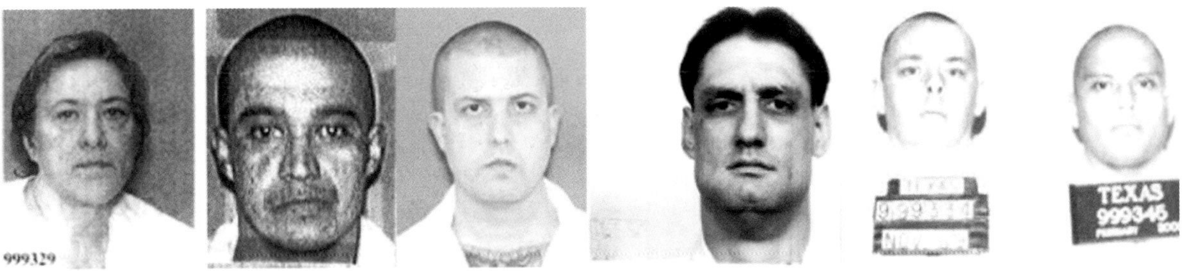
999329
TEXAS
999345

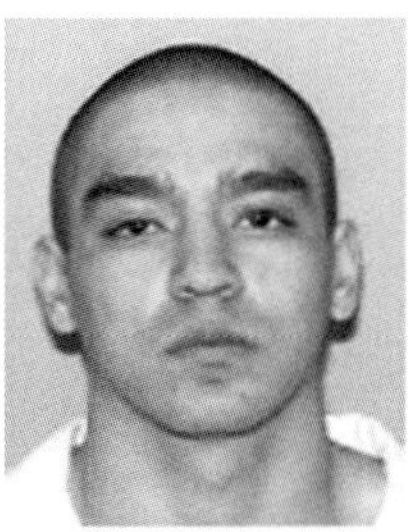

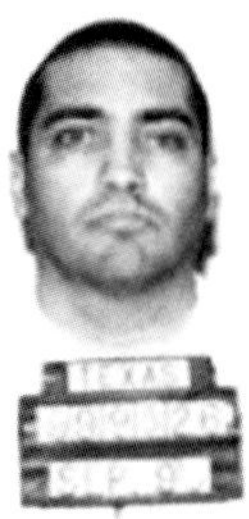

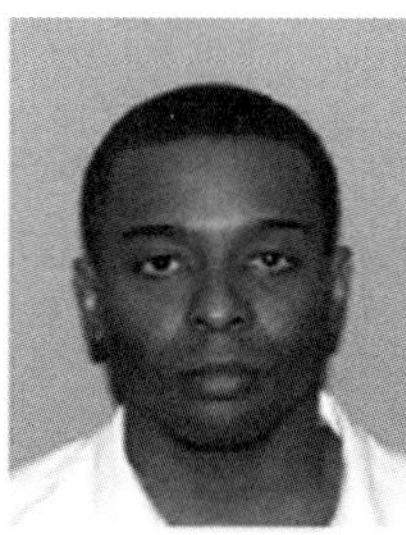

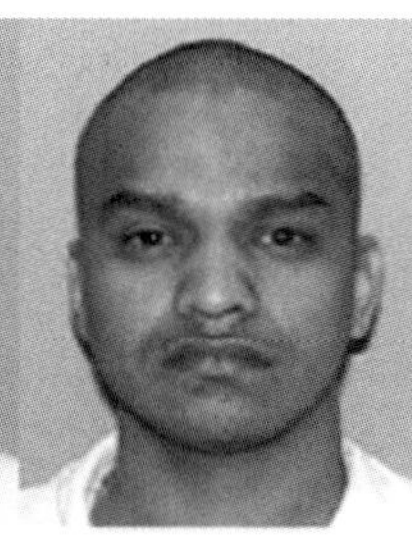

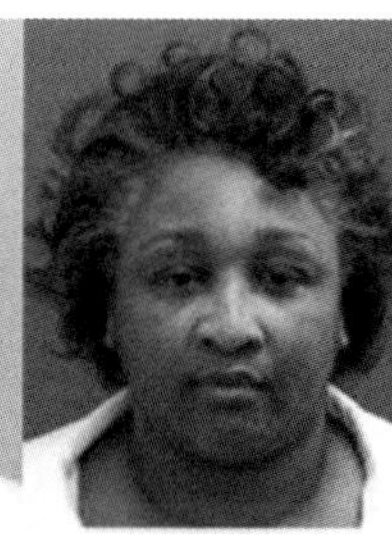

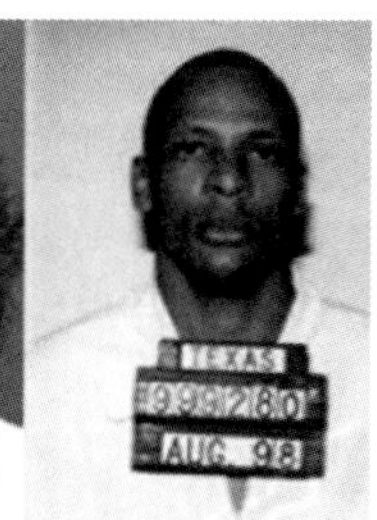
TEXAS
999280
AUG 98

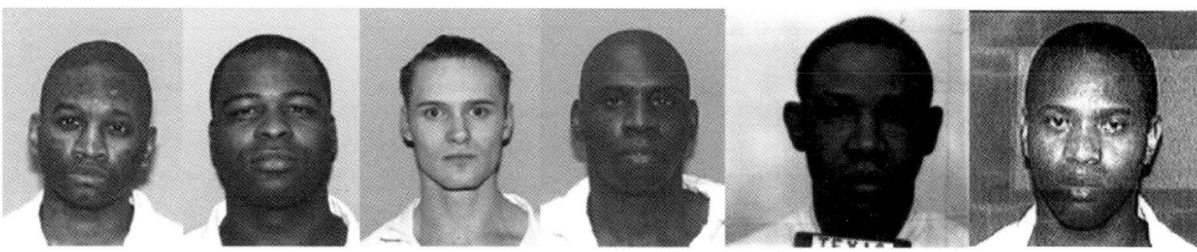

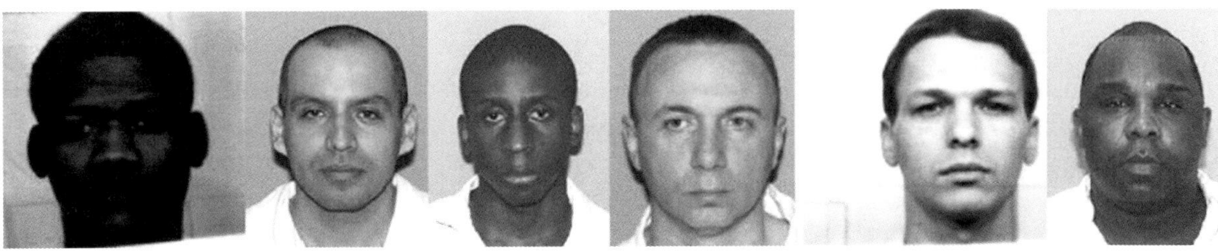

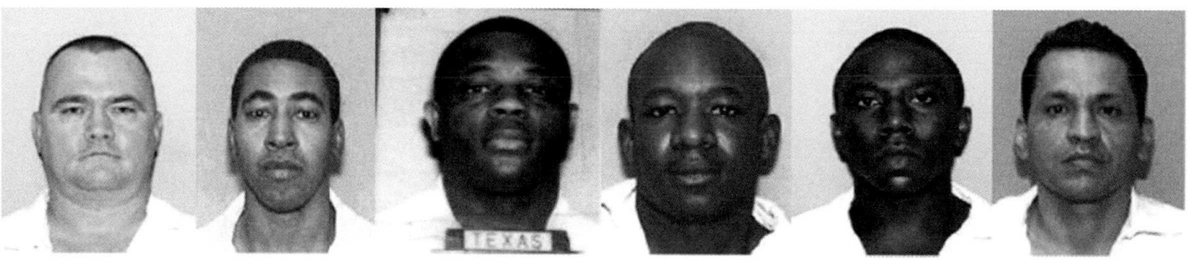
TEXAS

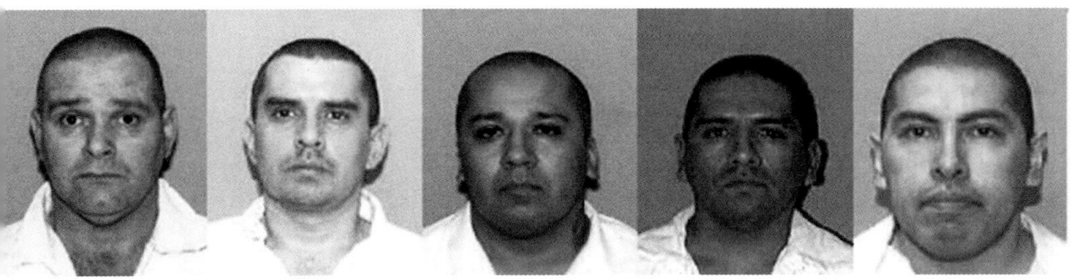

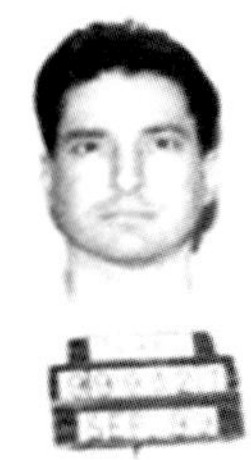

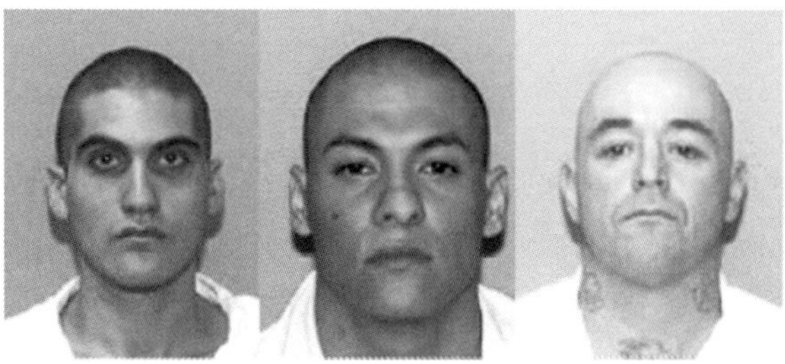

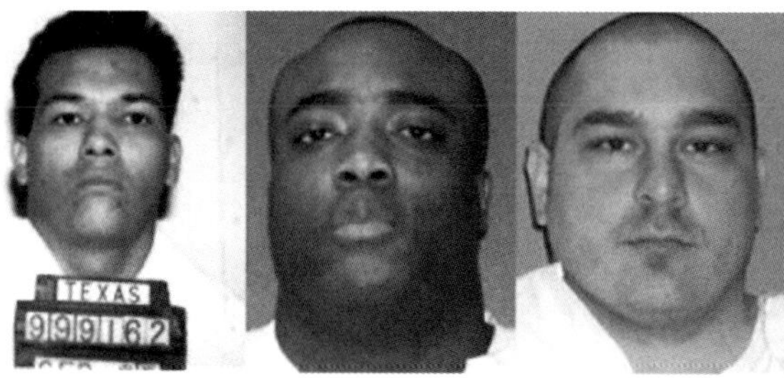
TEXAS
999162

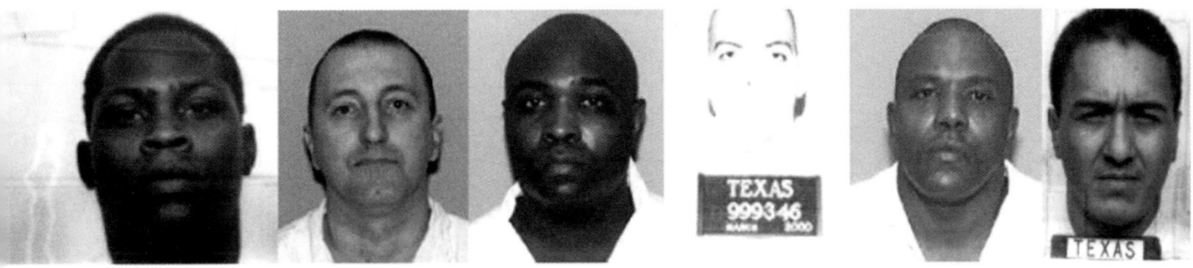
TEXAS
999346
TEXAS

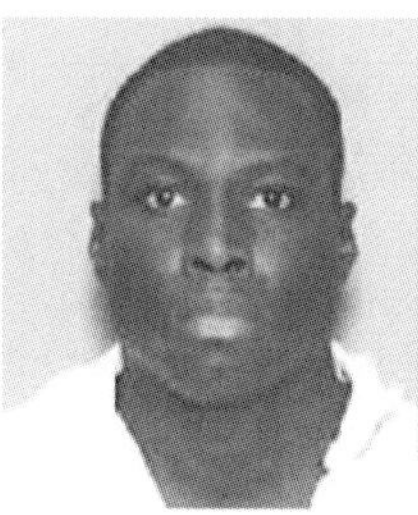
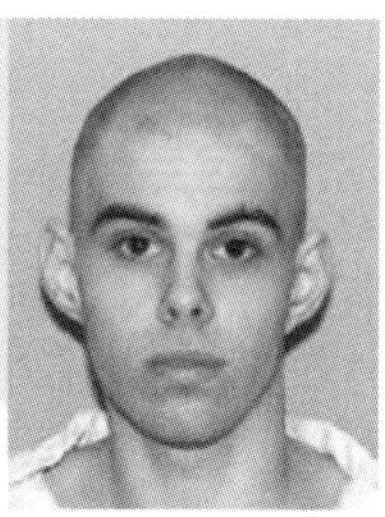
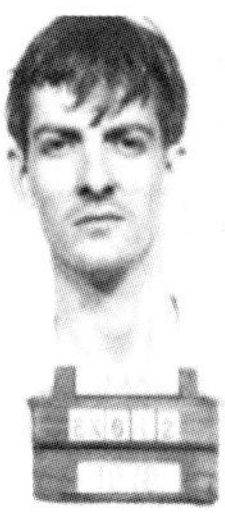
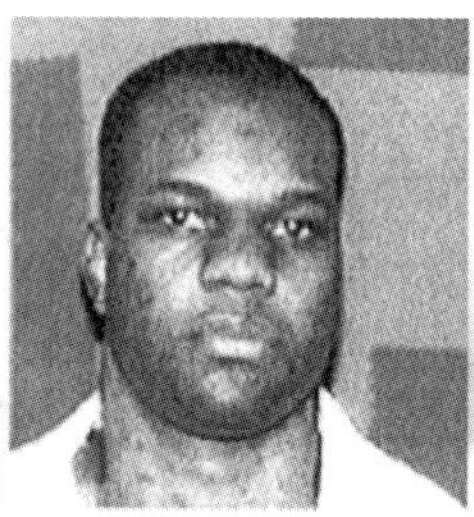
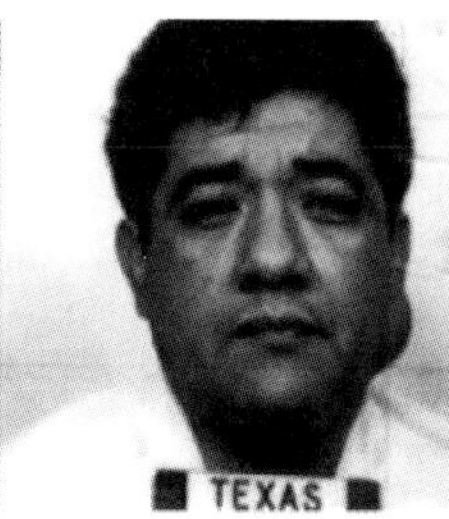
TEXAS
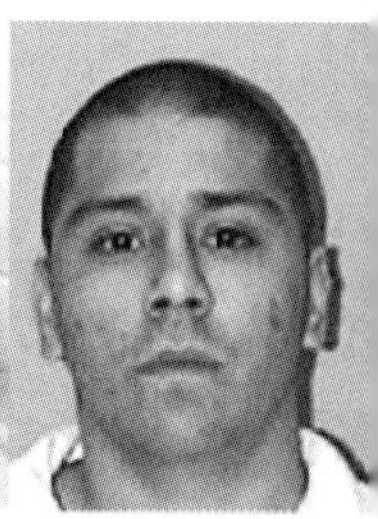

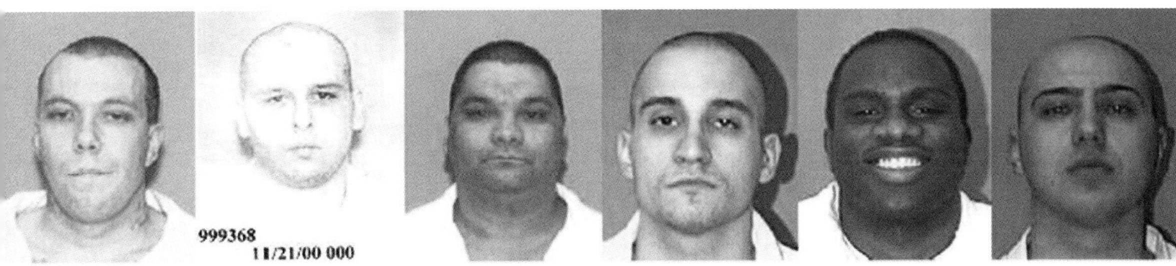
999368
11/21/00 000

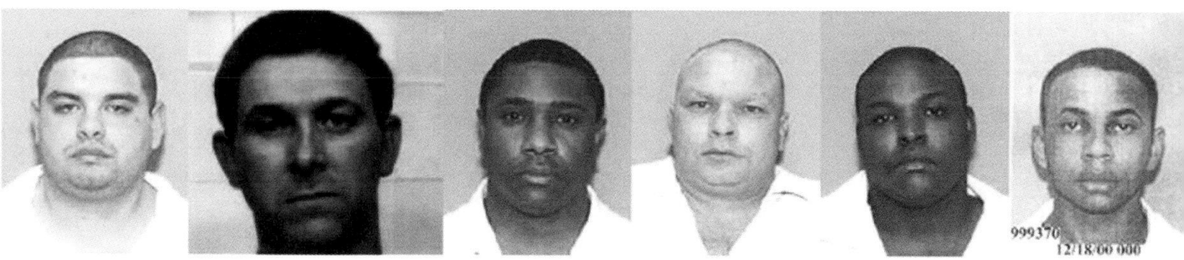
999370
12/18/00 000

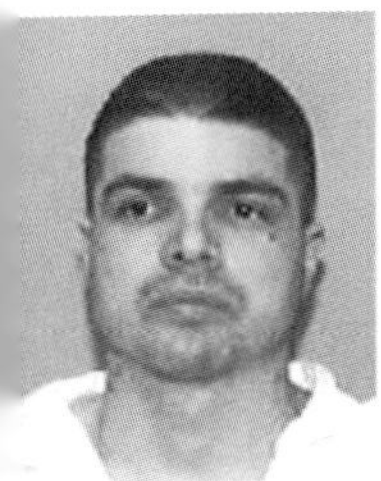
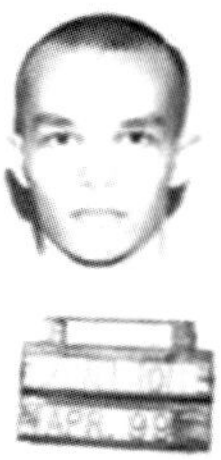
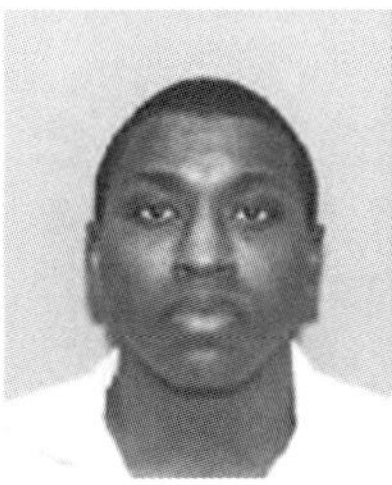
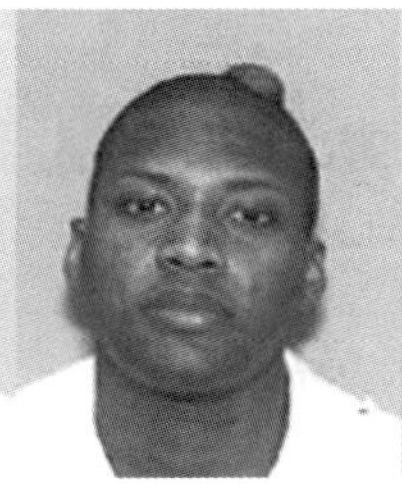
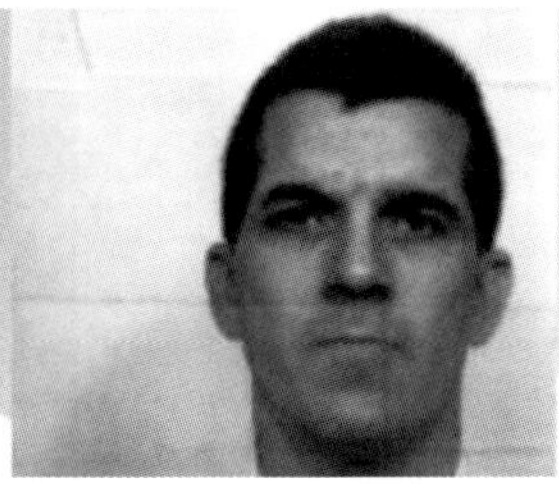
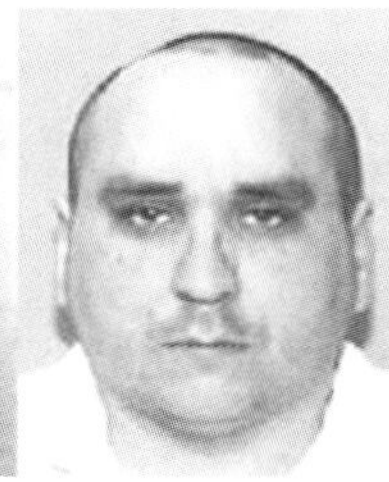

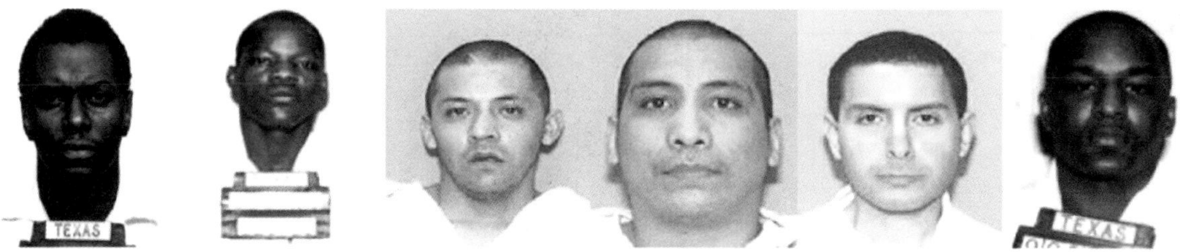
TEXAS
TEXAS

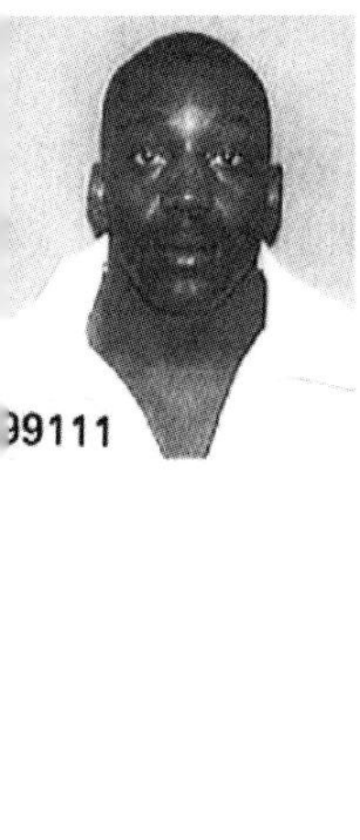
99111

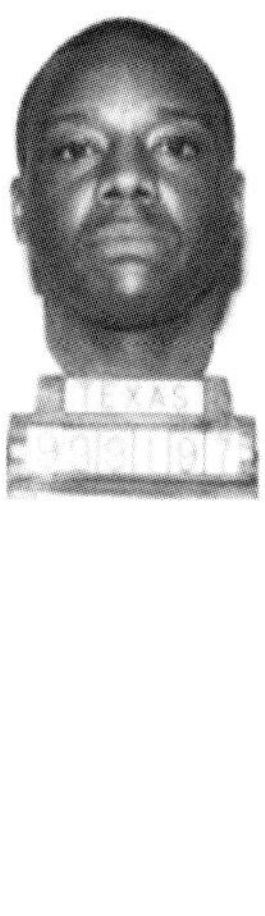
TEXAS

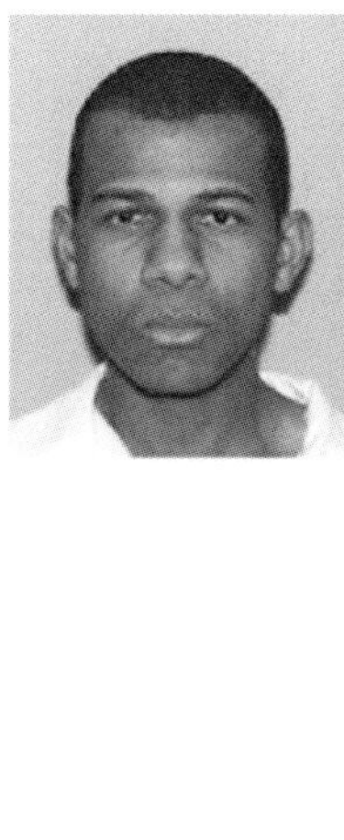

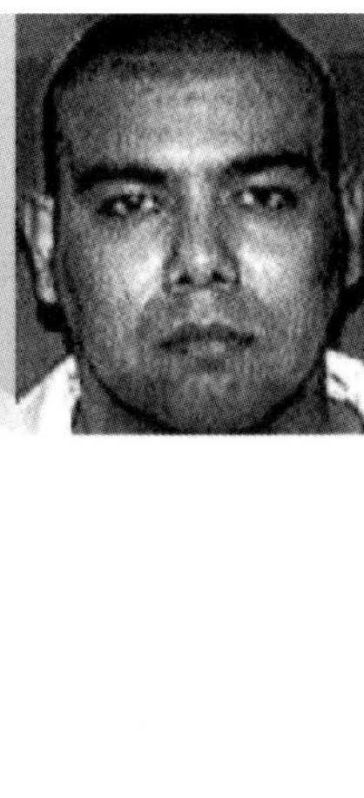

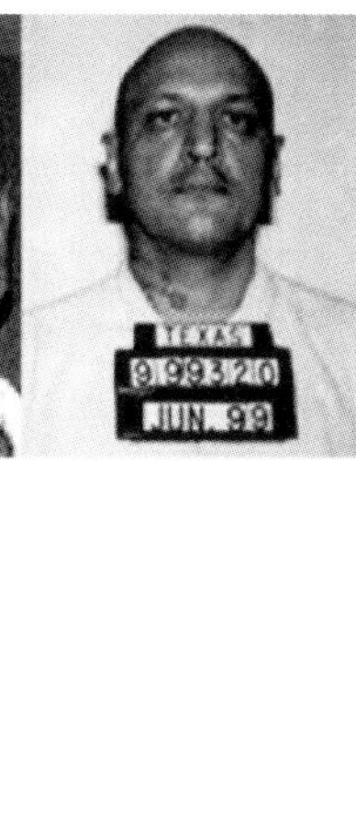
TEXAS
999320
JUN 99

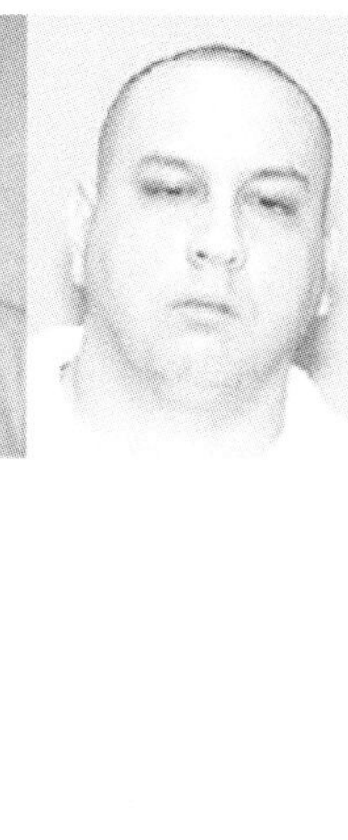

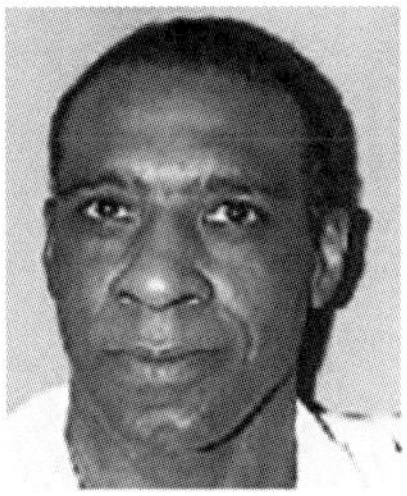

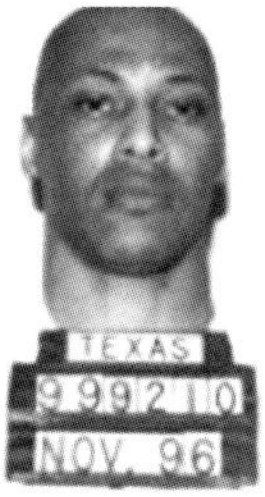

TEXAS
999210
NOV. 96

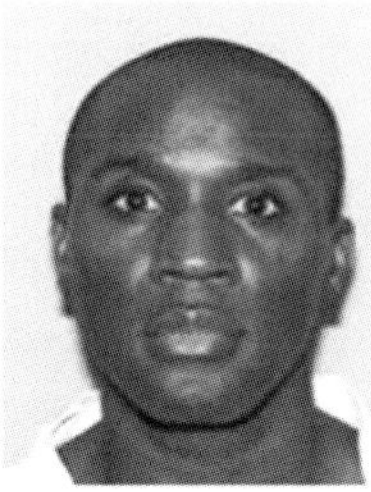

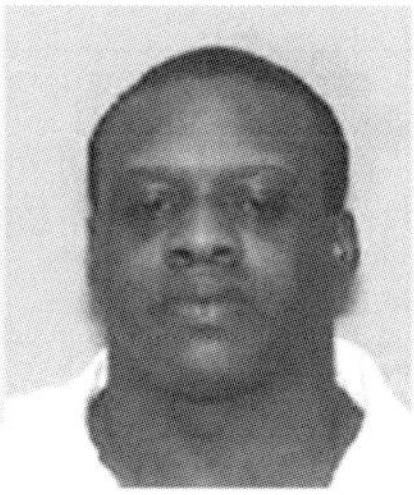

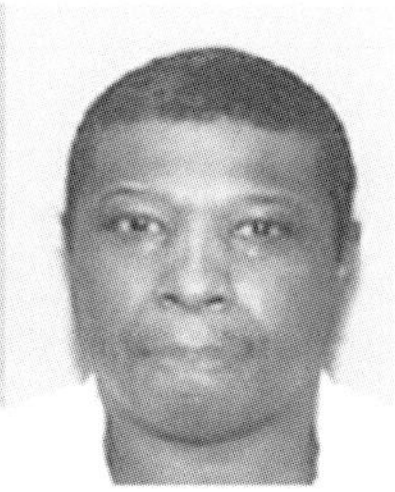

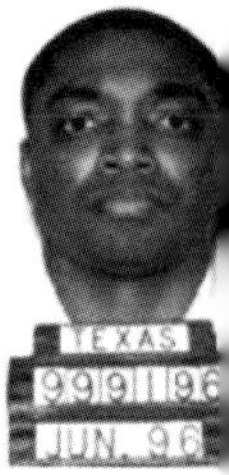

TEXAS
999I196
JUN. 96

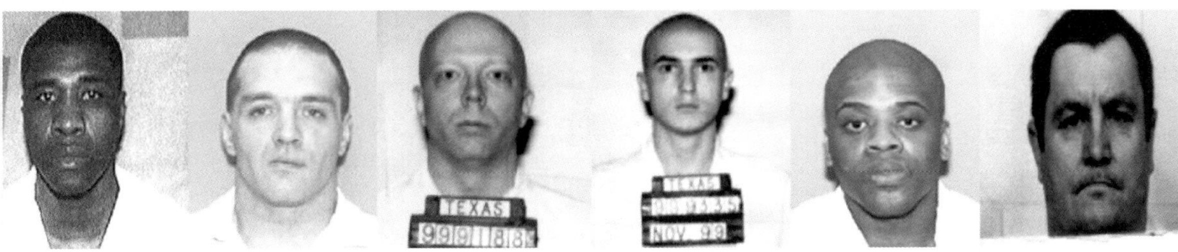
TEXAS
TEXAS
NOV 99

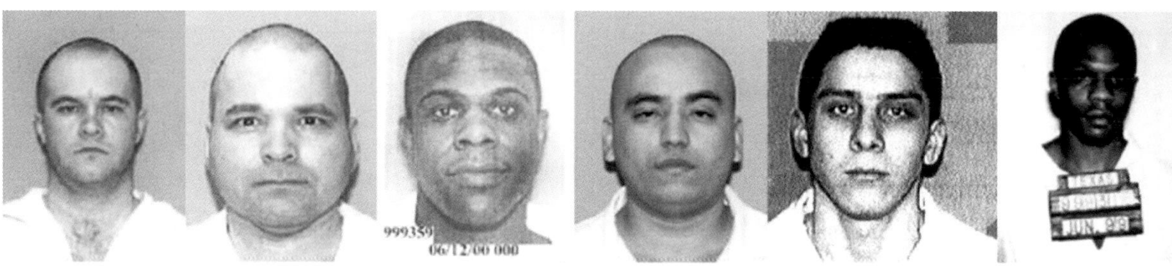
999359
06/12/00 000

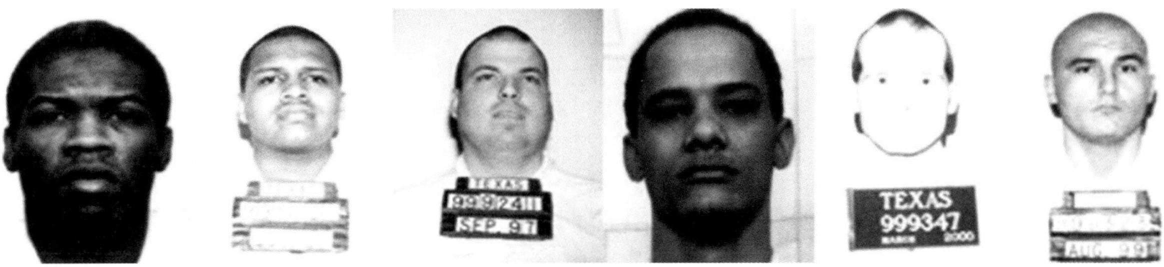
TEXAS
SEP 97
TEXAS
999347
2000

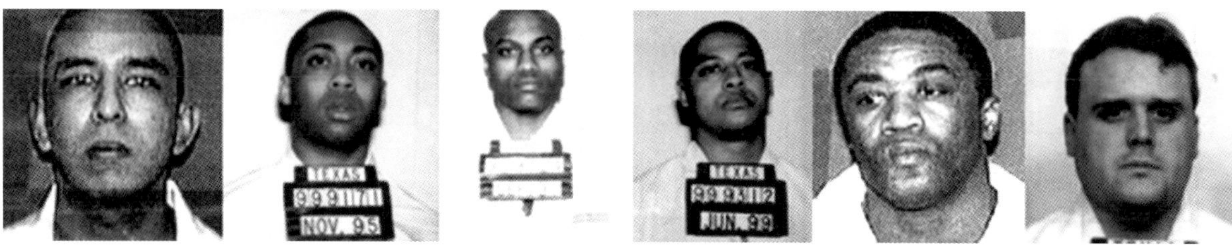
TEXAS
NOV. 95
TEXAS
999312
JUN 99

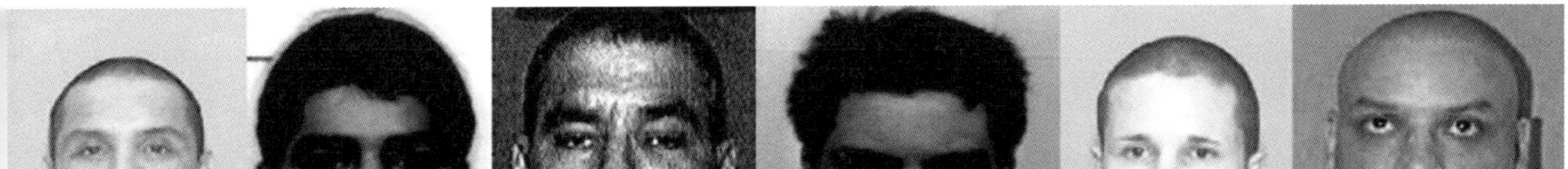

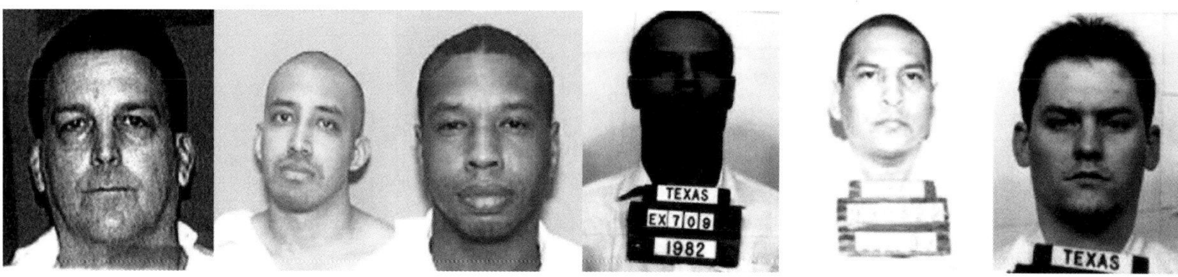
TEXAS
EX709
1982
TEXAS

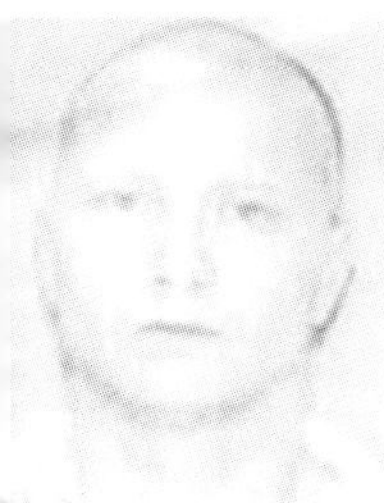

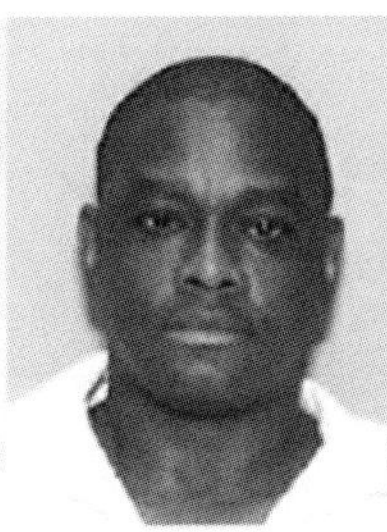

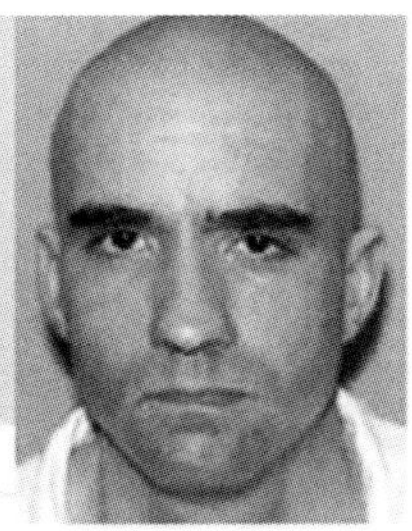

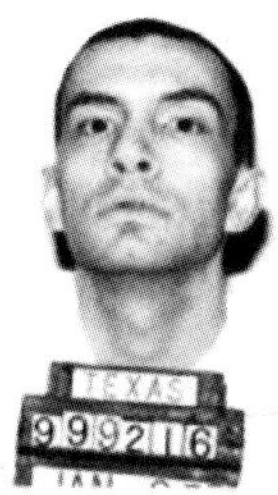
TEXAS
999216

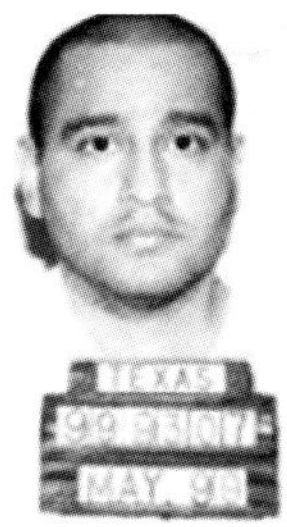
TEXAS

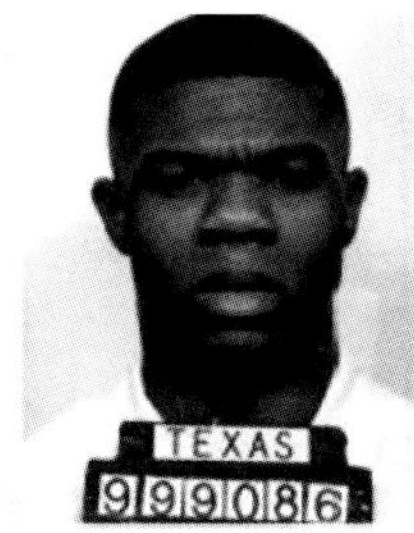
TEXAS
999086

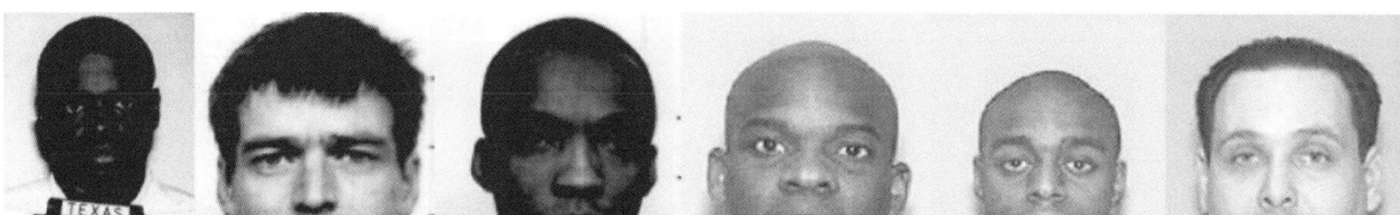
TEXAS
999206
SEP 96

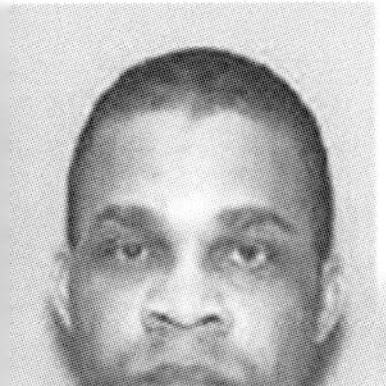

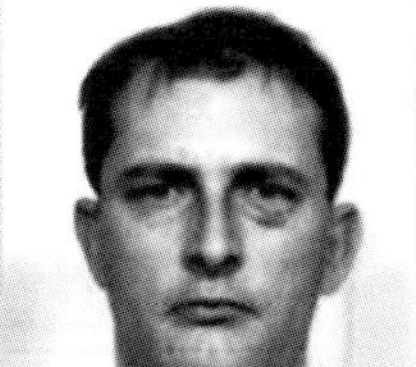
TEXAS

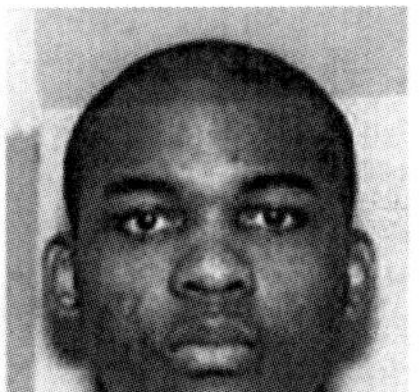

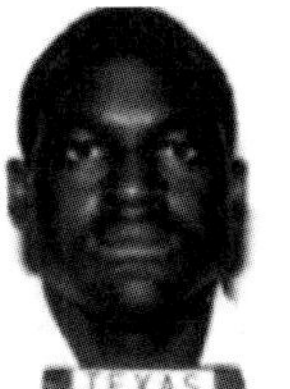
TEXAS
999131
NOV. 94

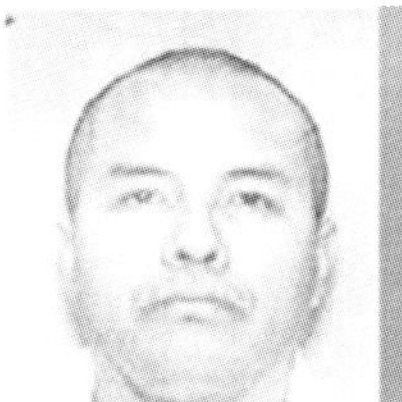
999356
05/24/00 000

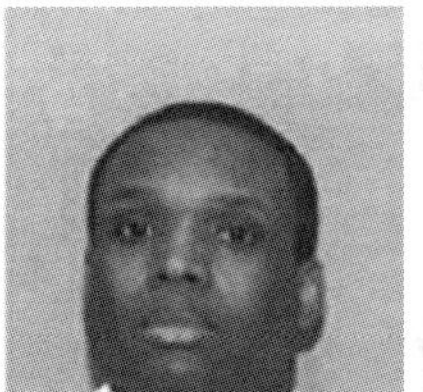

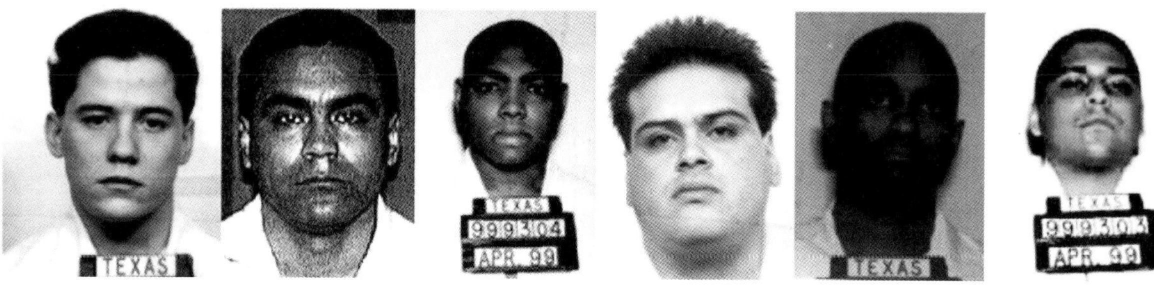
TEXAS
TEXAS
999304
APR 99
TEXAS
TEXAS
999303
APR 99

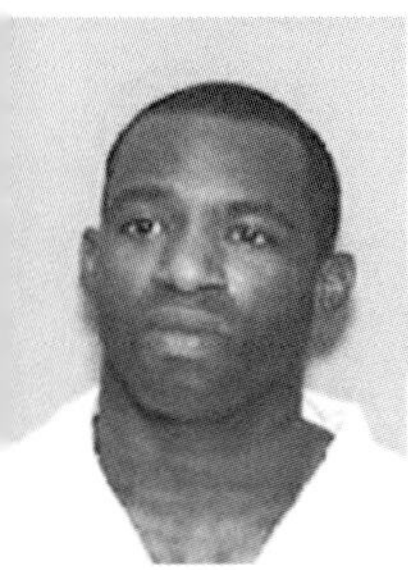

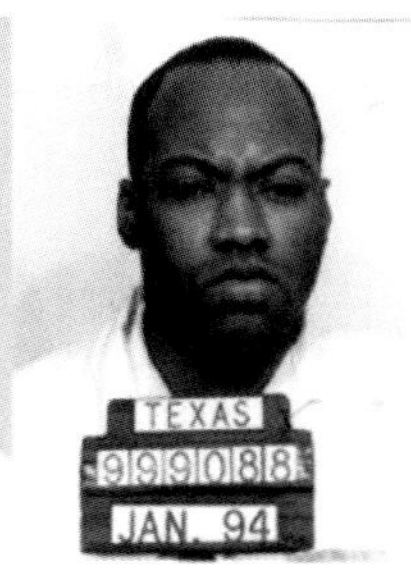

TEXAS
999088
JAN. 94

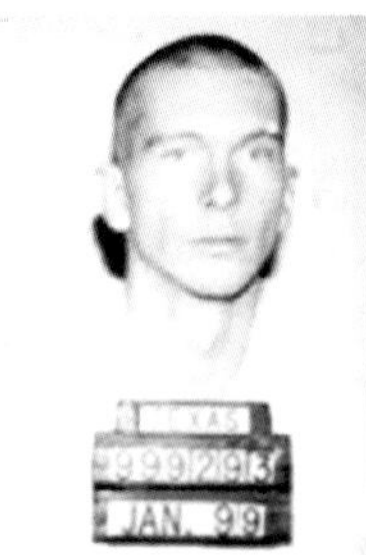

999293
JAN. 99

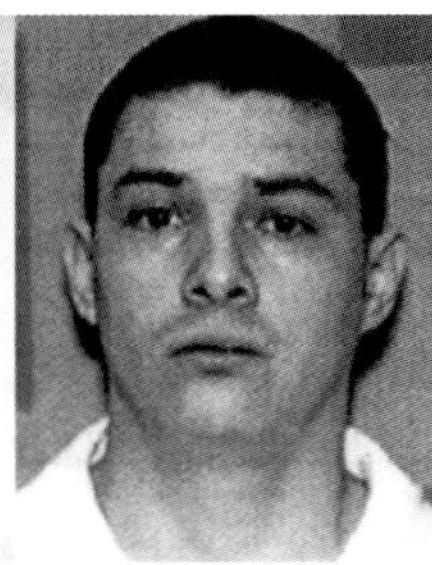

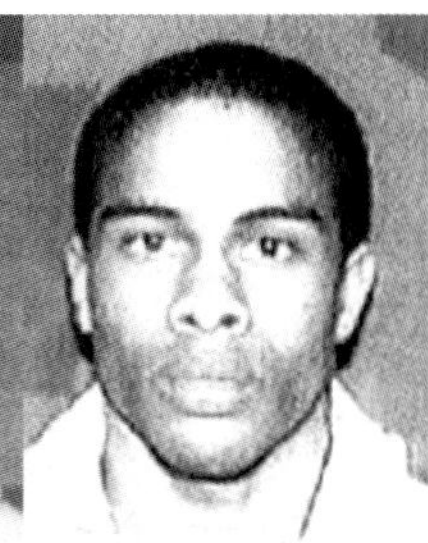

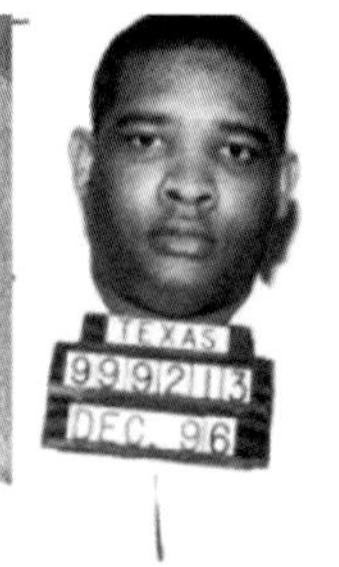

TEXAS
999213
DEC. 96

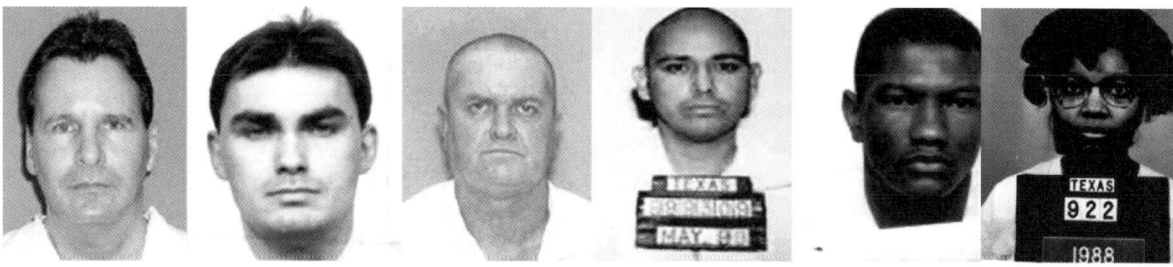
TEXAS
TEXAS
922
1988

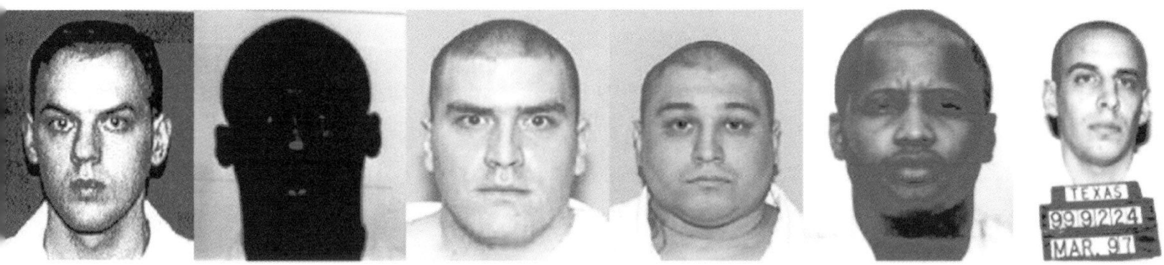
TEXAS
999224
MAR. 97

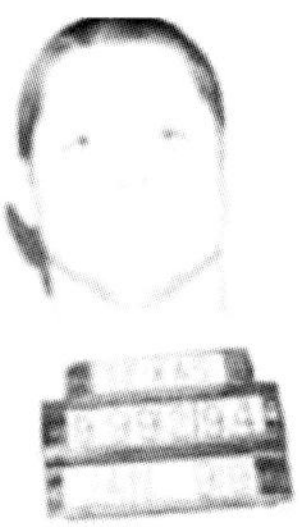
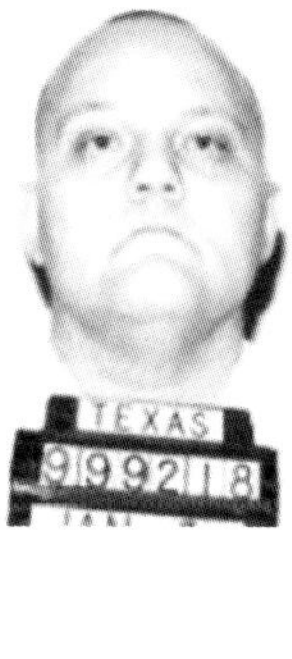
TEXAS
999218
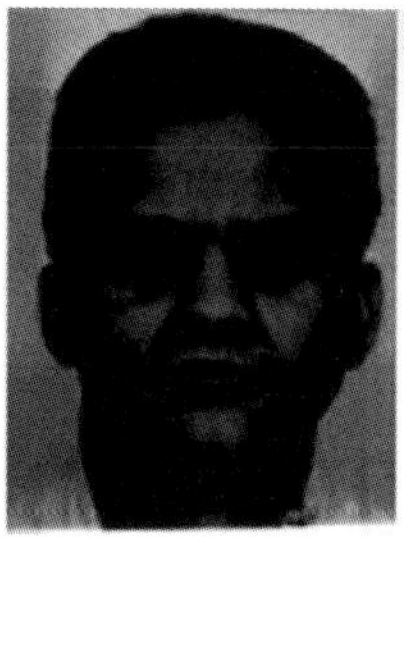
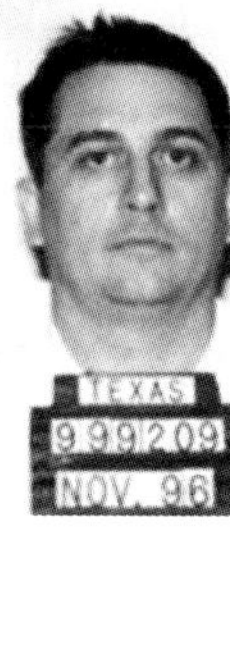
TEXAS
999209
NOV. 96
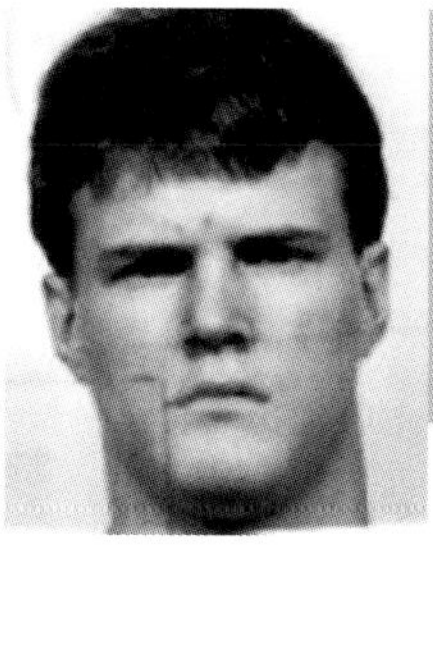
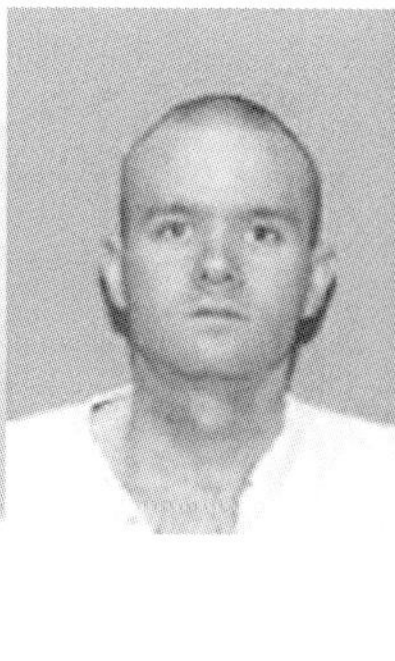

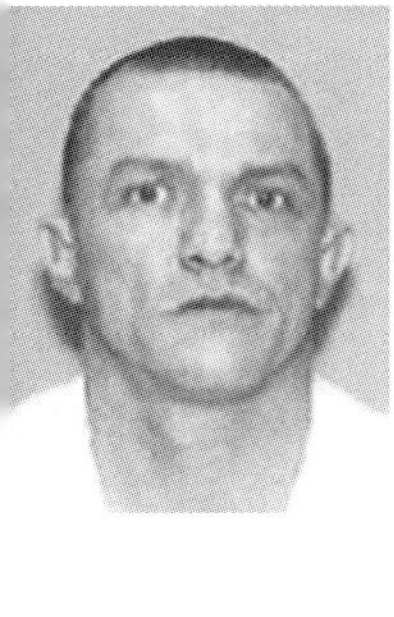
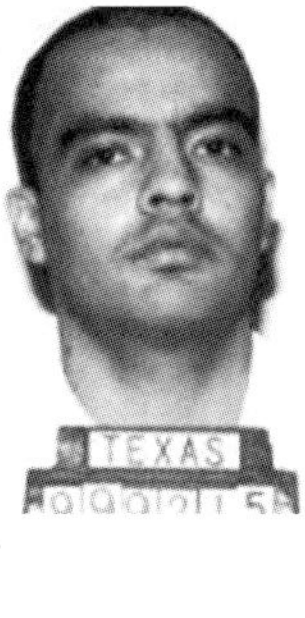
TEXAS
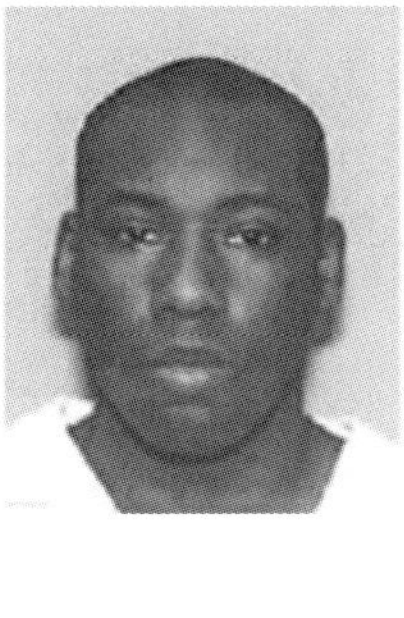
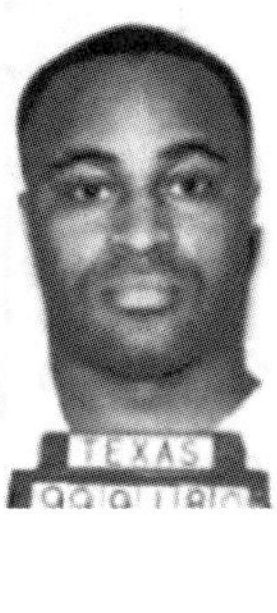
TEXAS
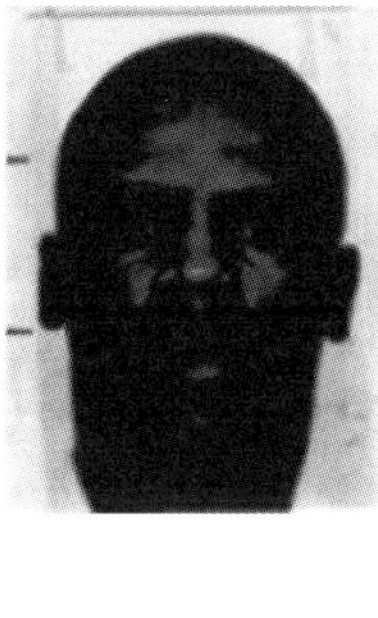
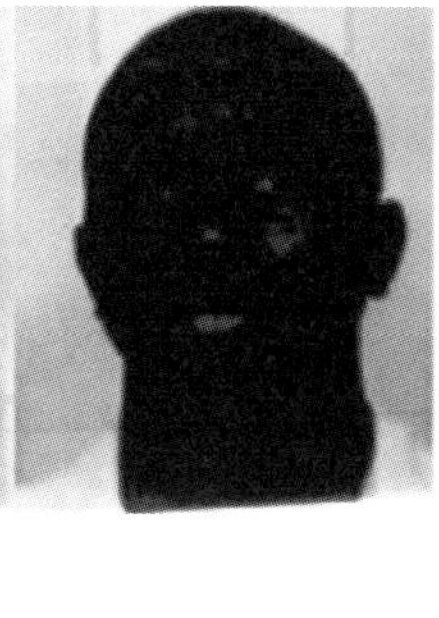

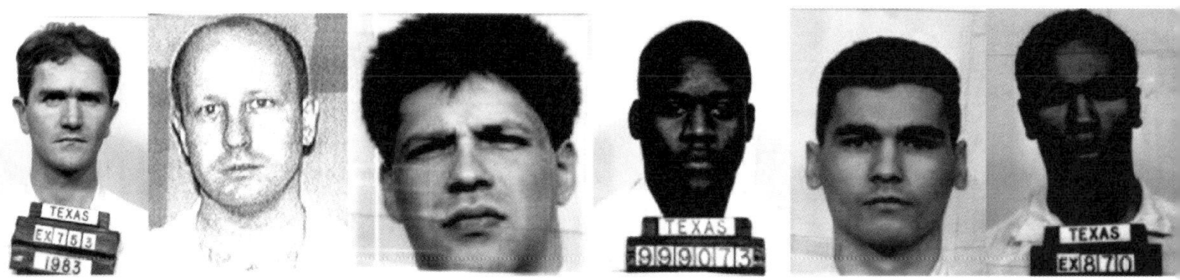
TEXAS
EX753
1983
TEXAS
999073
TEXAS
EX870

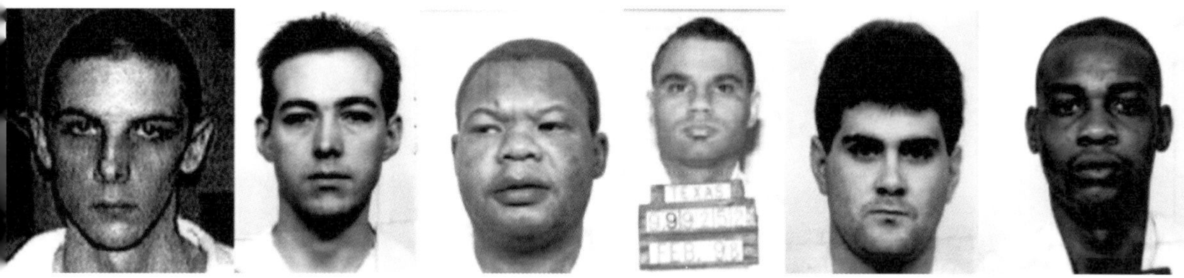
TEXAS

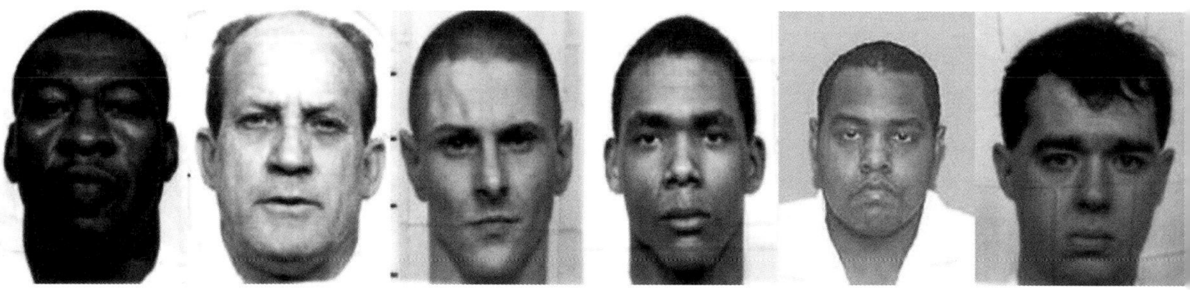

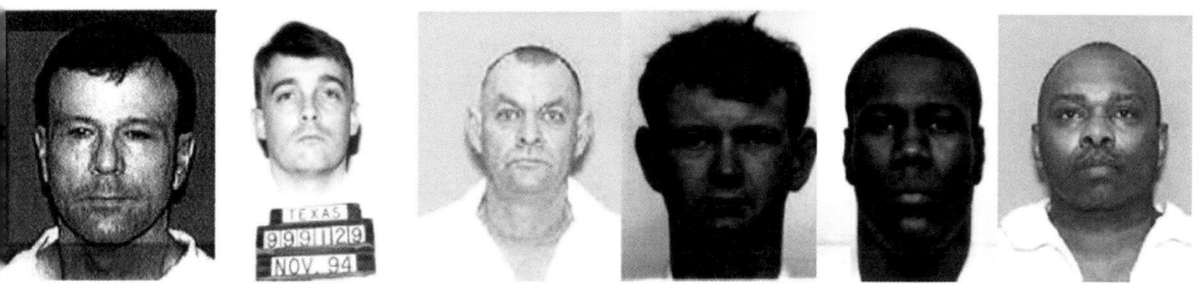
TEXAS
999129
NOV. 94

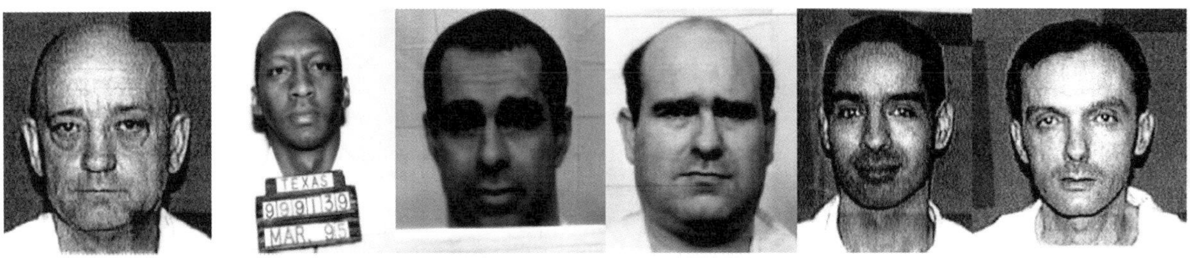
TEXAS
999139
MAR 95

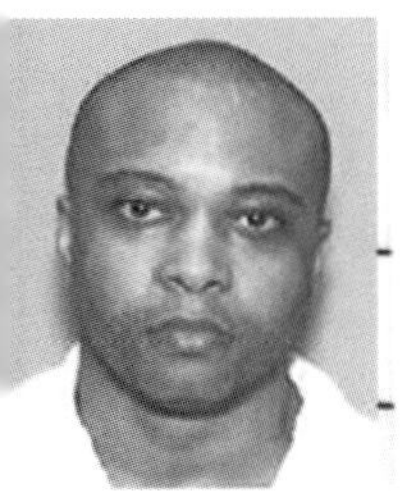
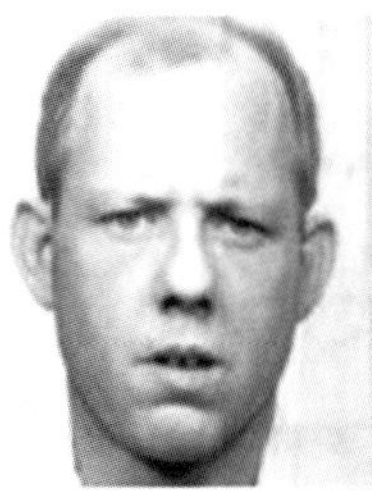
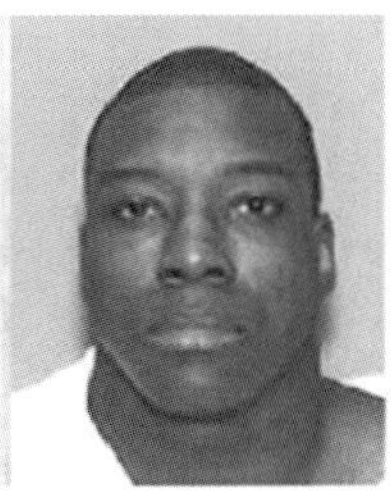
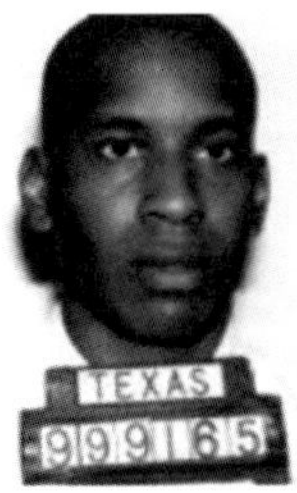
TEXAS
999165
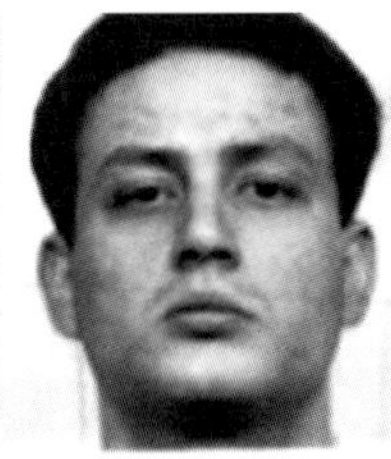
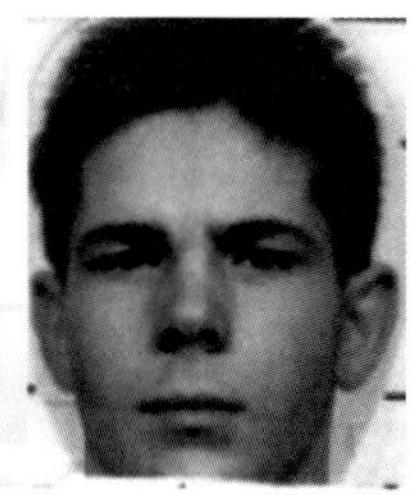

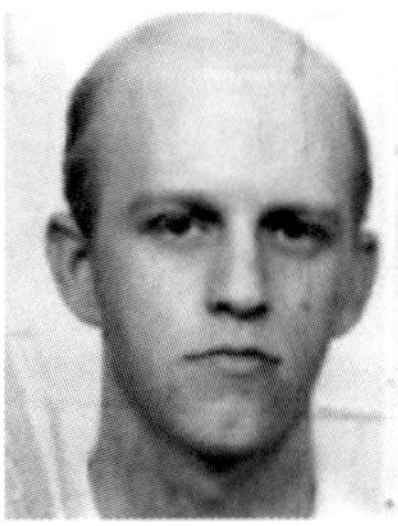

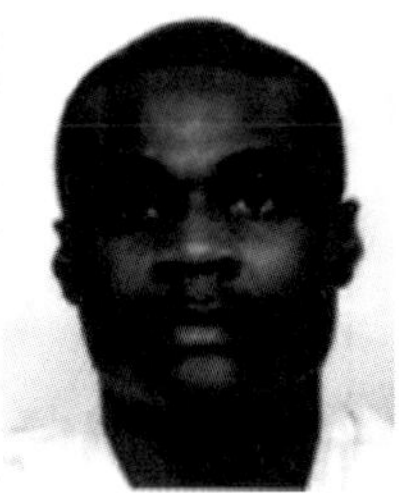

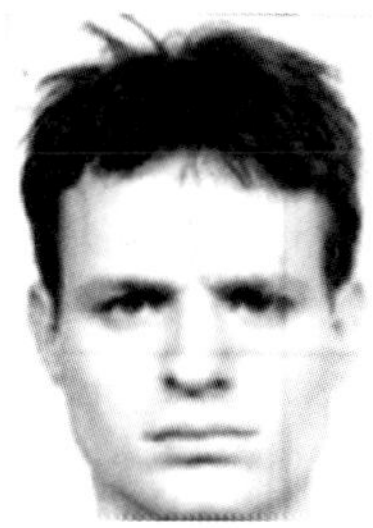

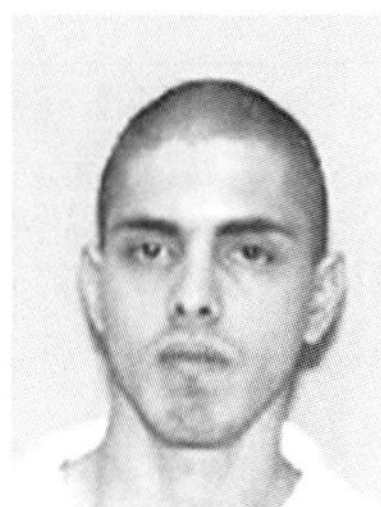

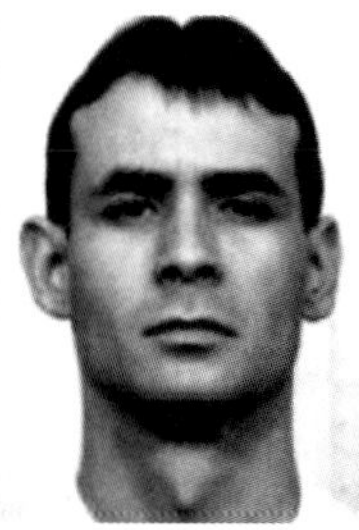

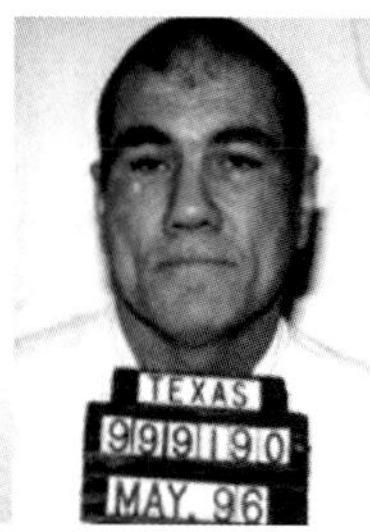
TEXAS
999190
MAY. 96

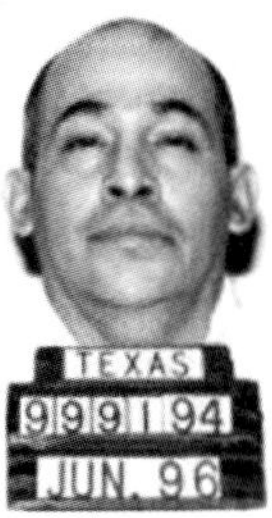
TEXAS
999194
JUN. 96

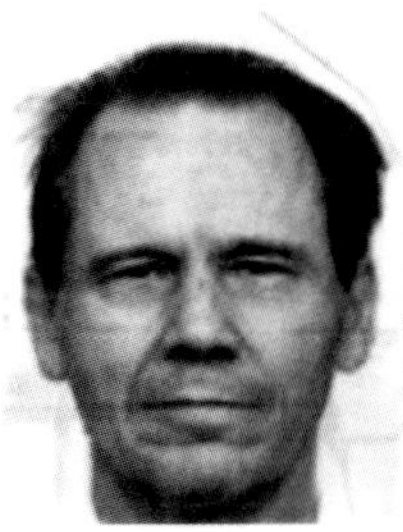

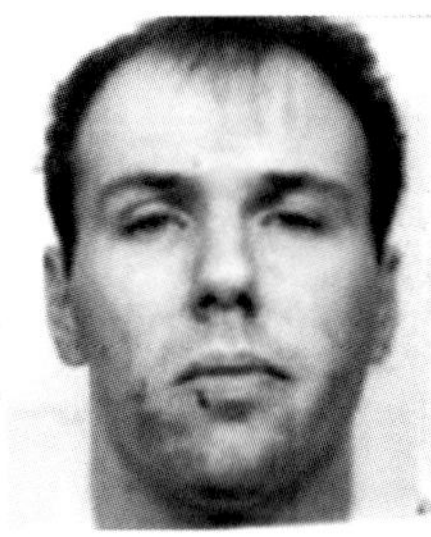

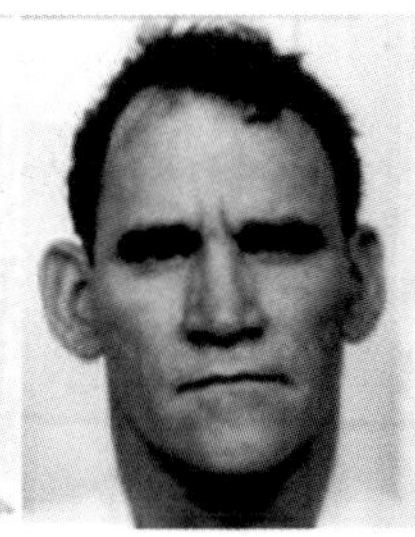

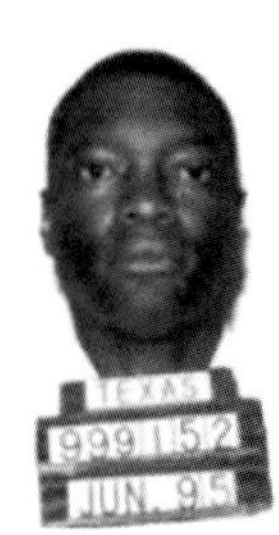
TEXAS
999152
JUN. 95

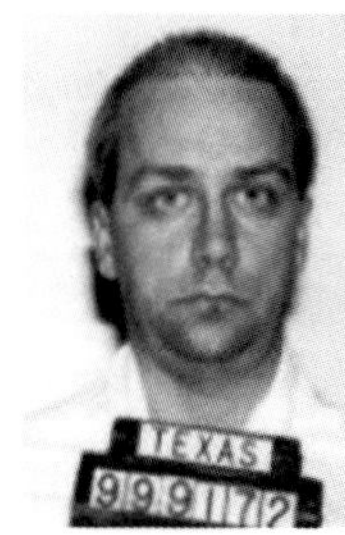
TEXAS
999172

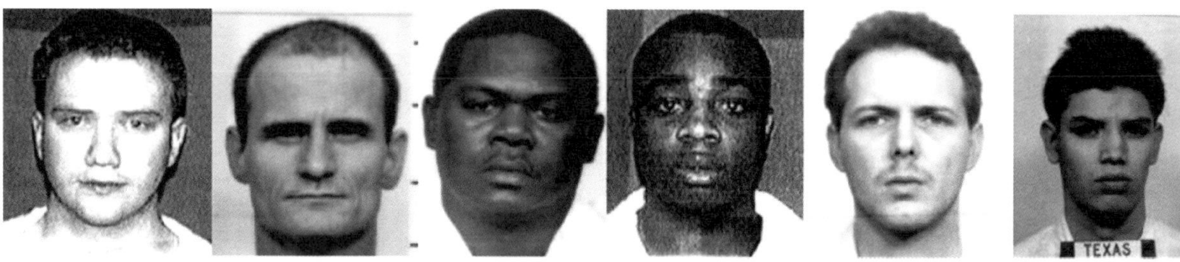
TEXAS

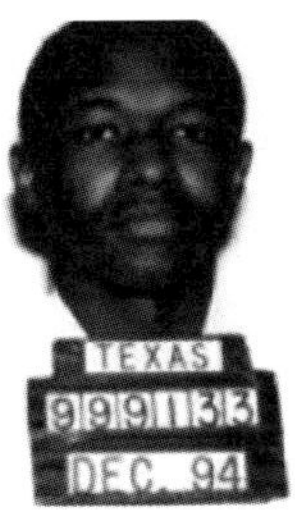
TEXAS
999133
DEC. 94

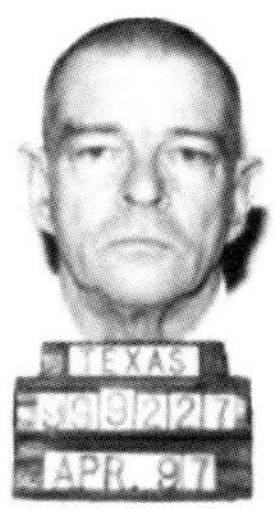
TEXAS
APR. 97

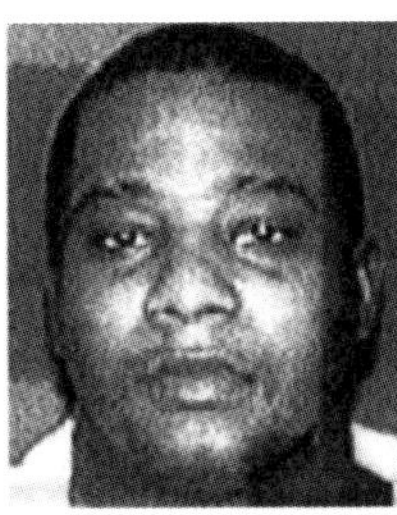

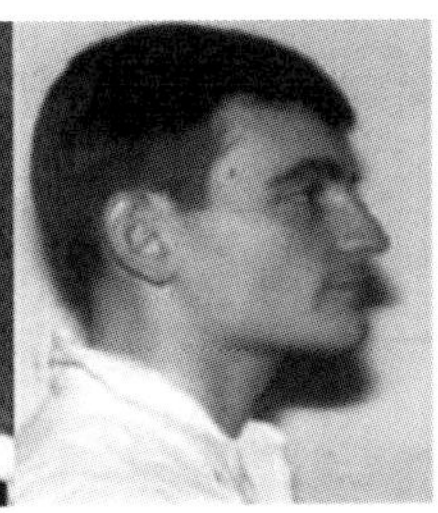

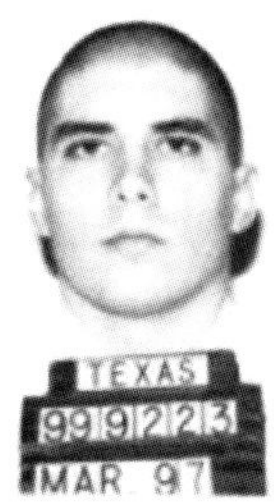
TEXAS
999223
MAR 97

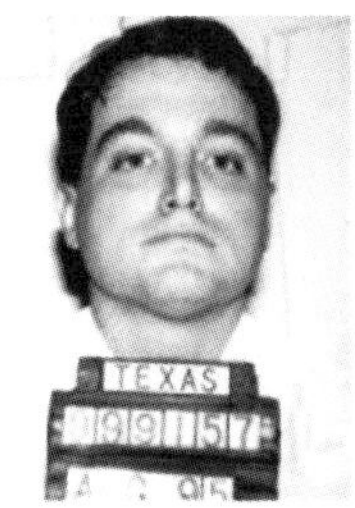
TEXAS

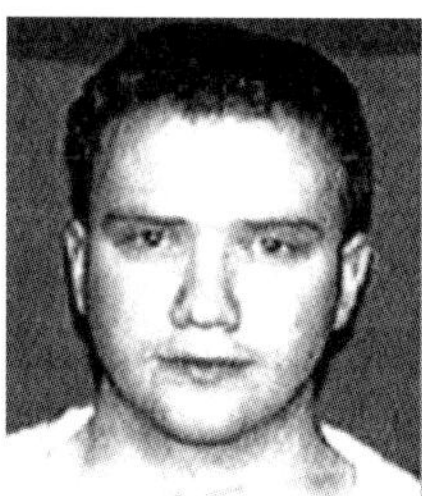
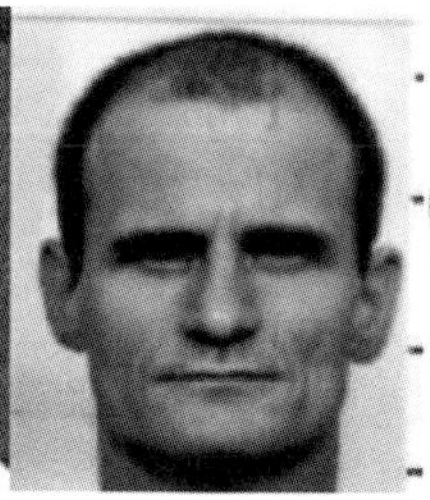
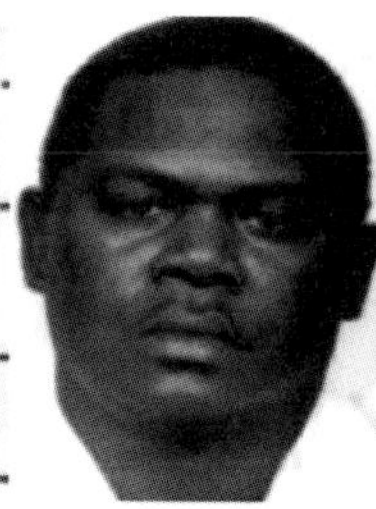
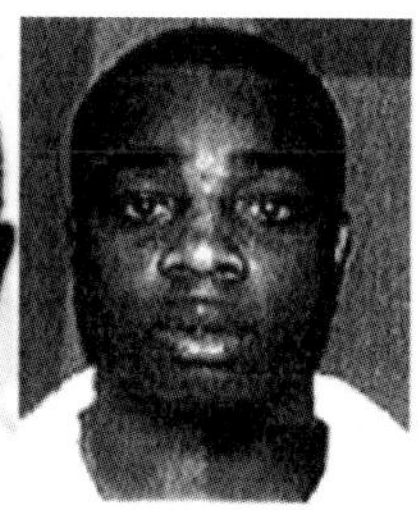
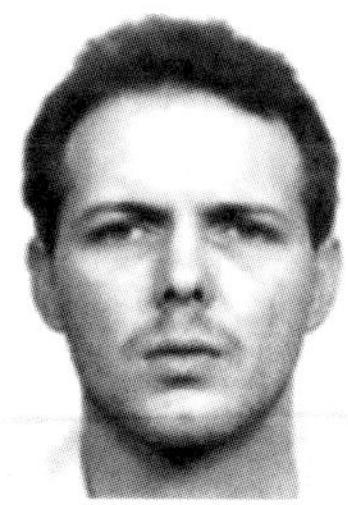
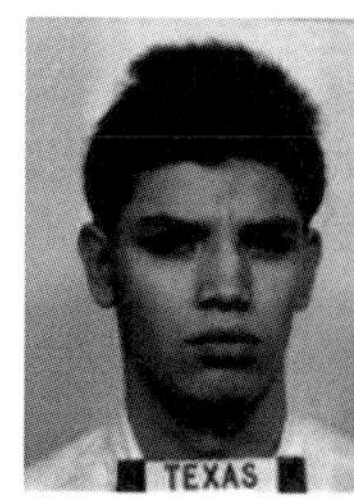
TEXAS

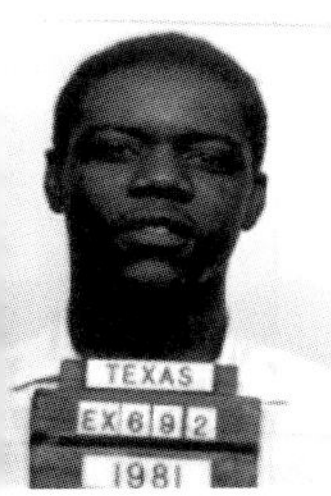
TEXAS
EX692
1981
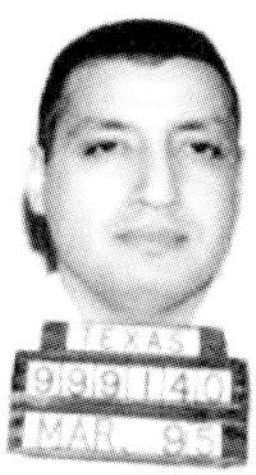
TEXAS
999140
MAR. 95
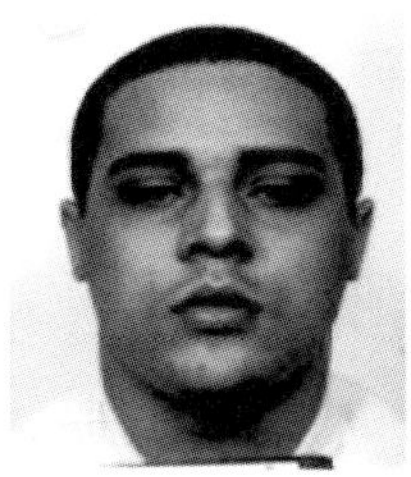
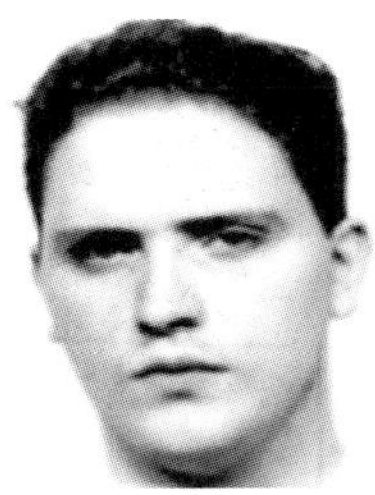
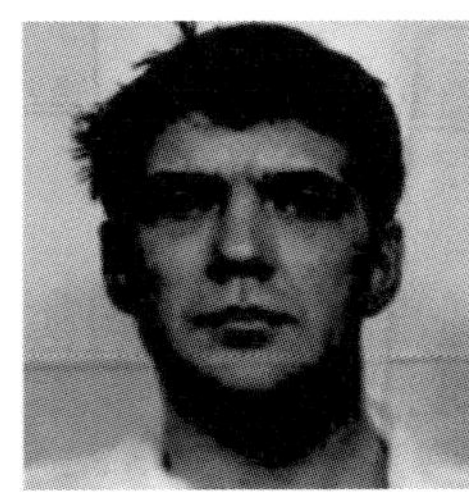
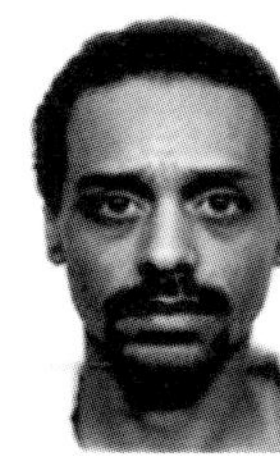

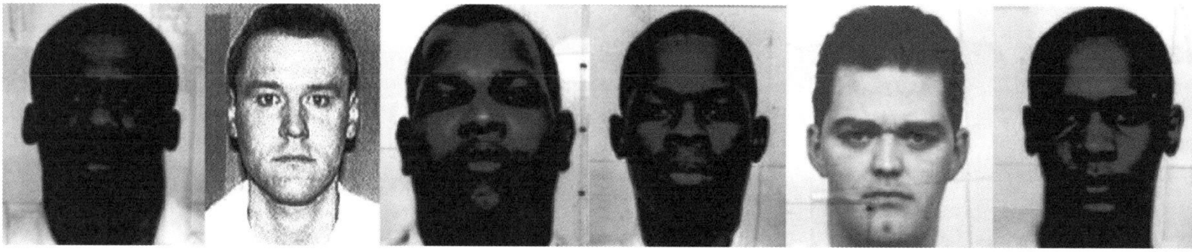

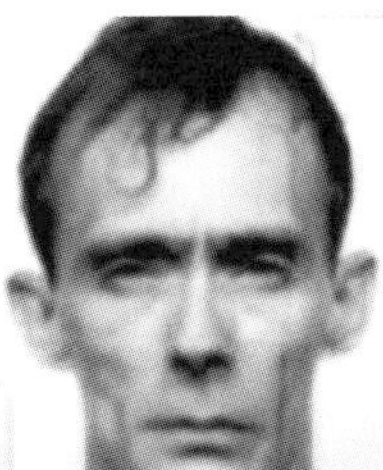
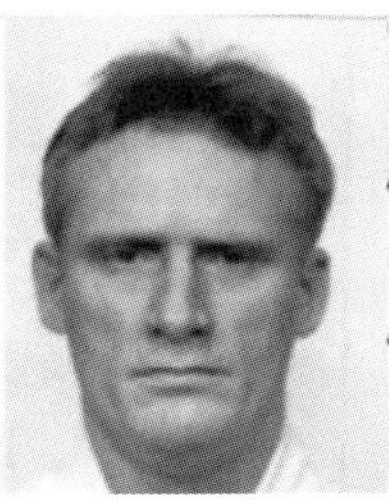
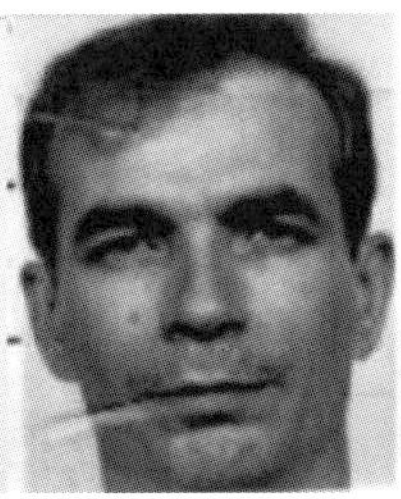
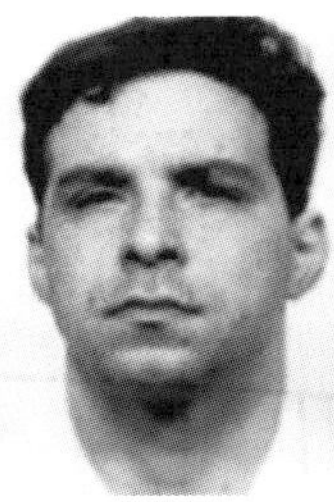
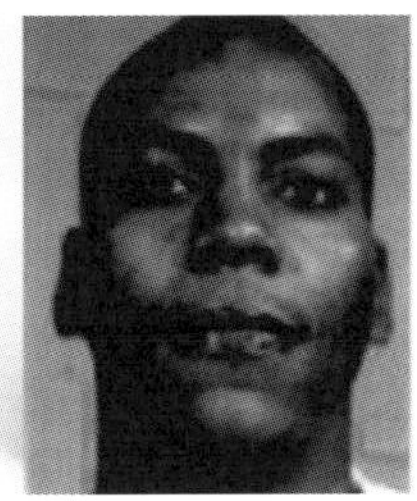
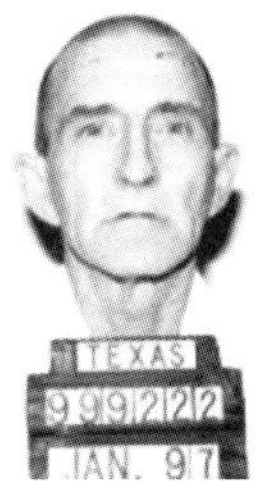
TEXAS
999222
JAN. 97

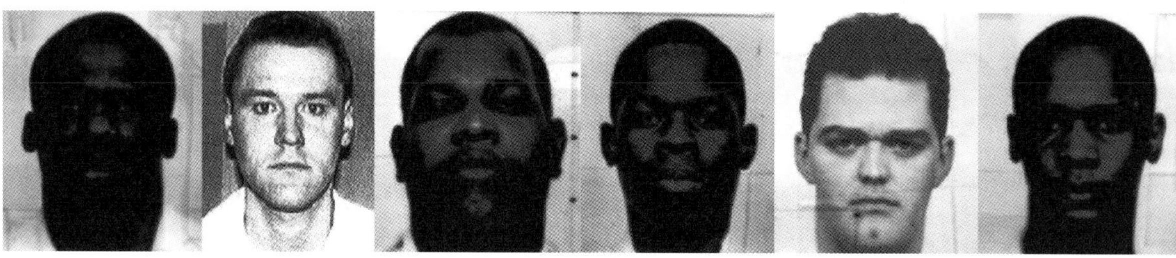

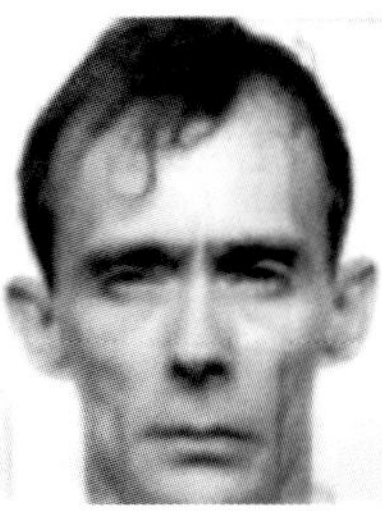
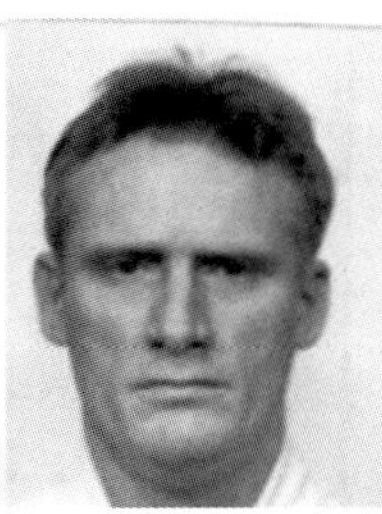
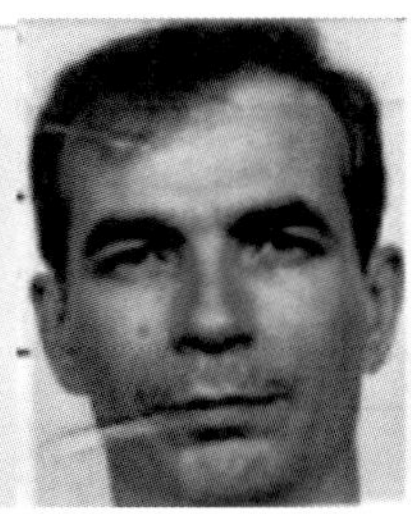
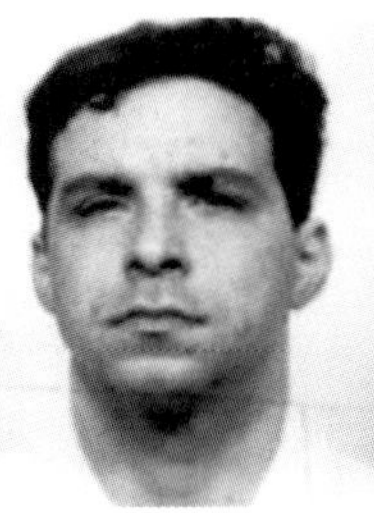
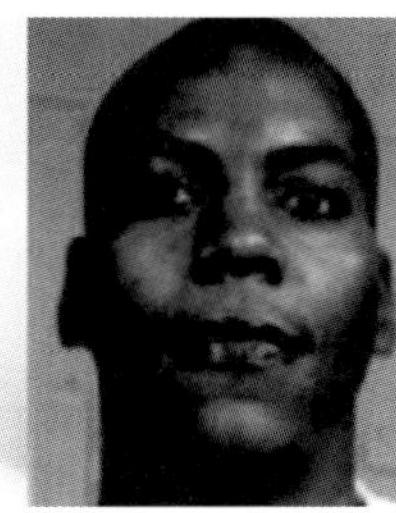
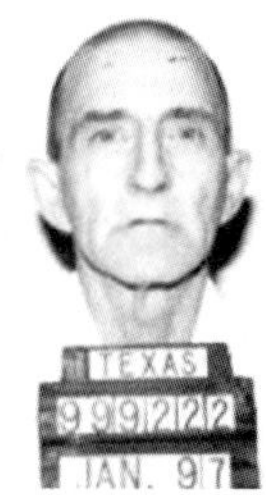
TEXAS
999222
JAN. 97

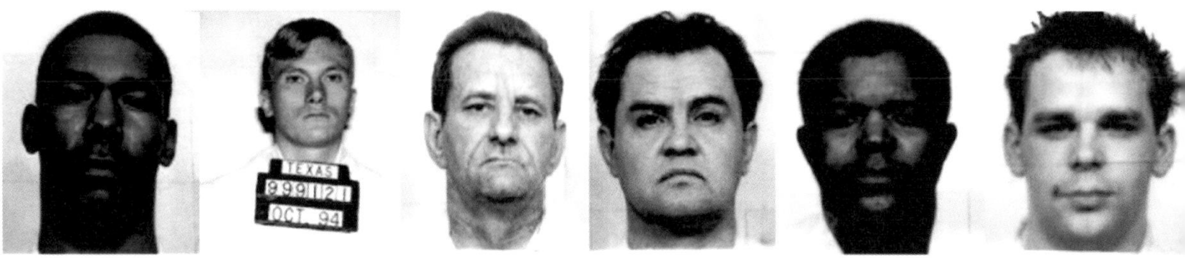
TEXAS
999121
OCT 94

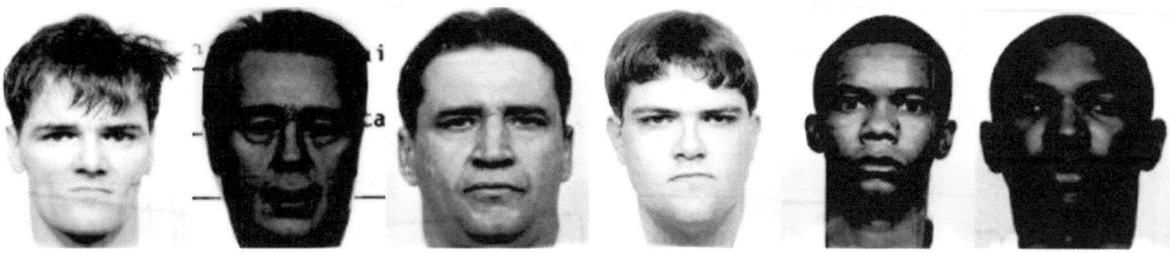

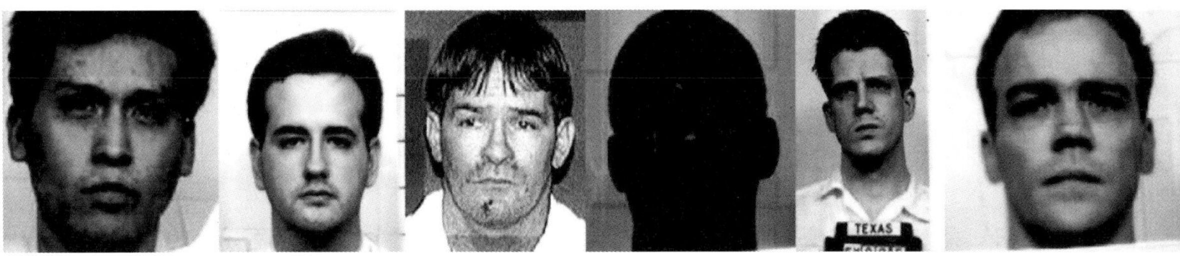
TEXAS

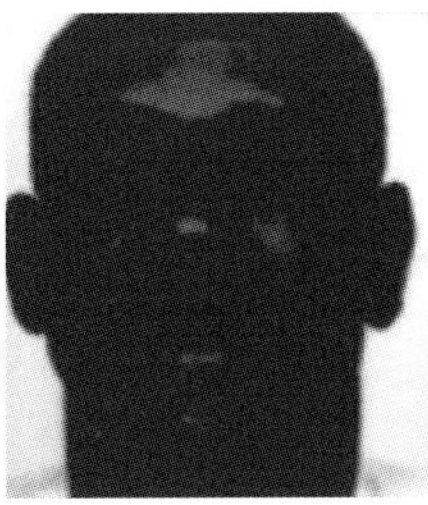
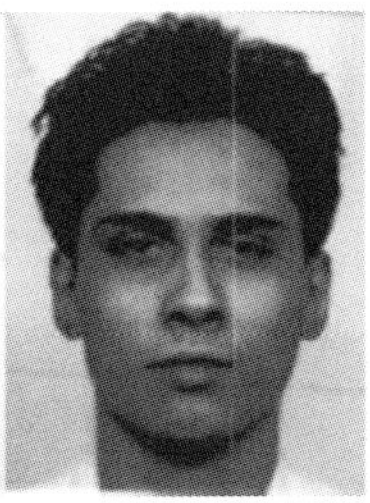
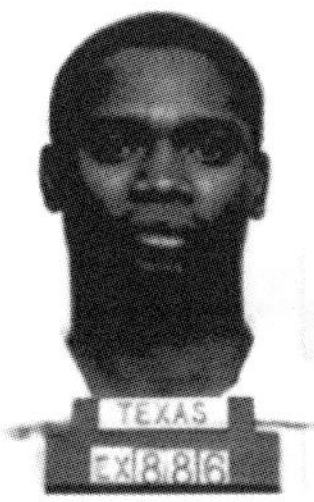
TEXAS
EX 886
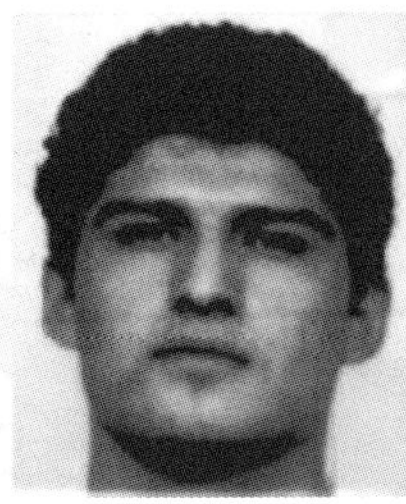
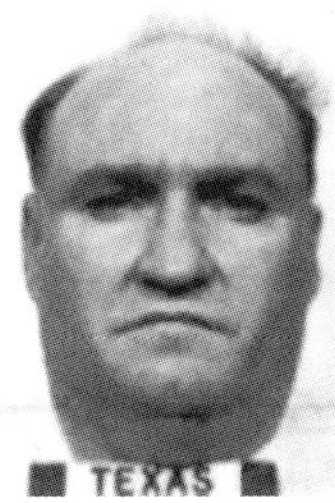
TEXAS
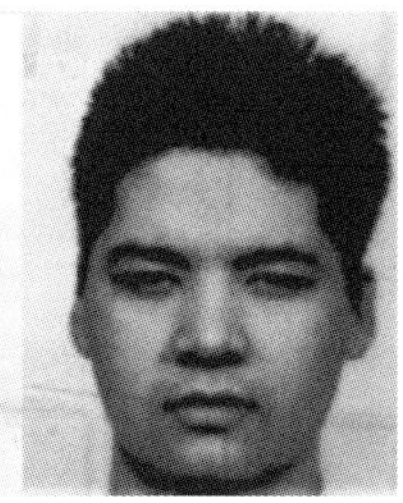

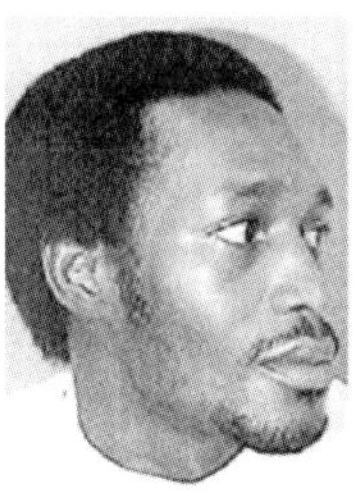

01/06/99 001

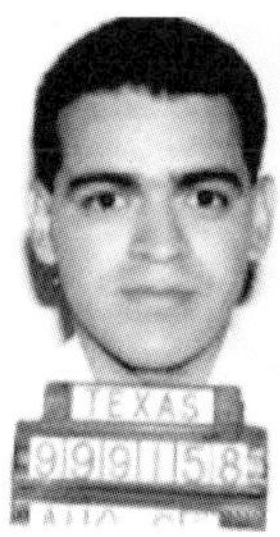

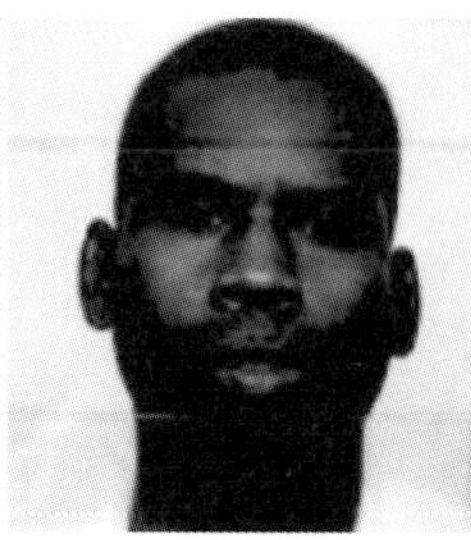

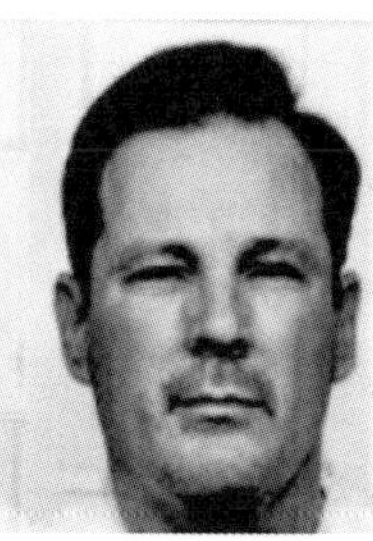

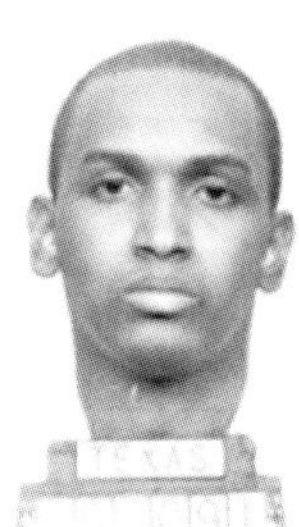

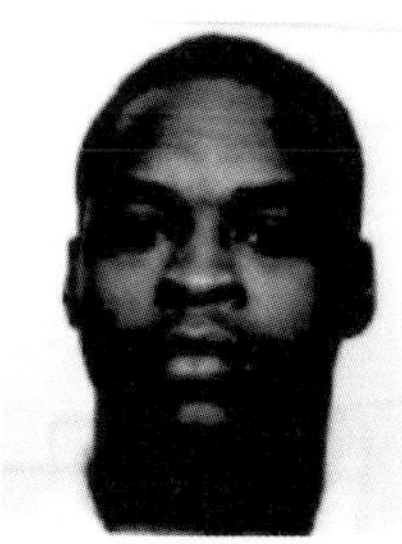

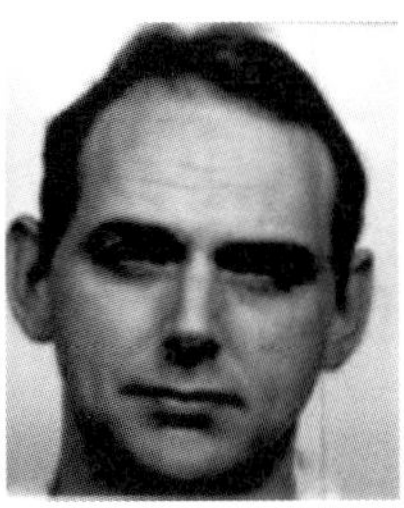
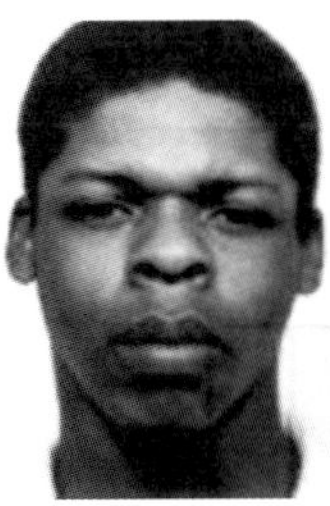
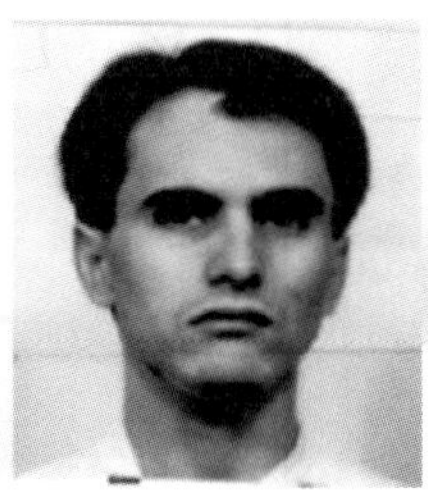
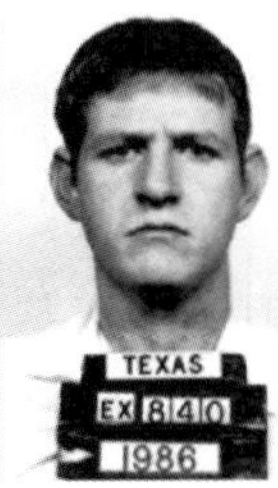
TEXAS
EX 840
1986
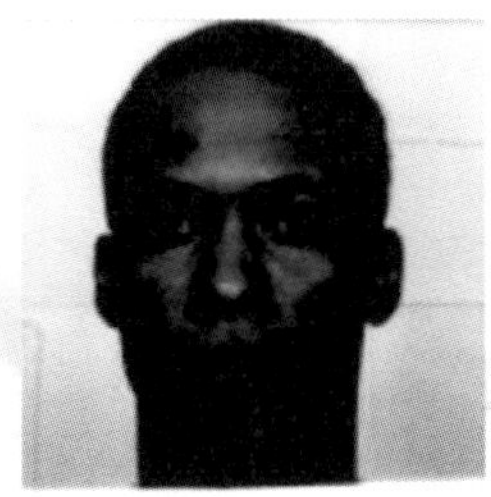
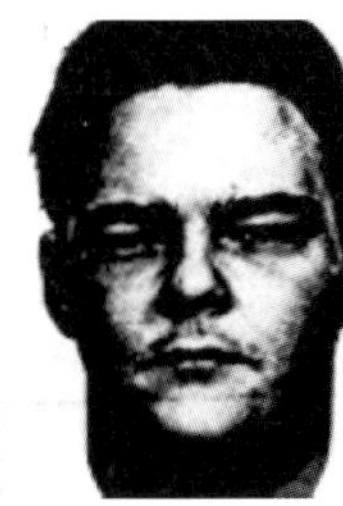

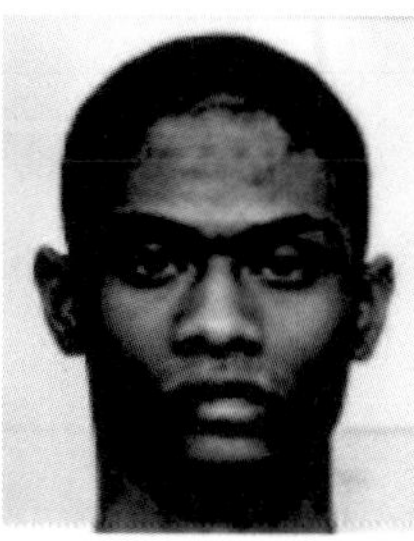

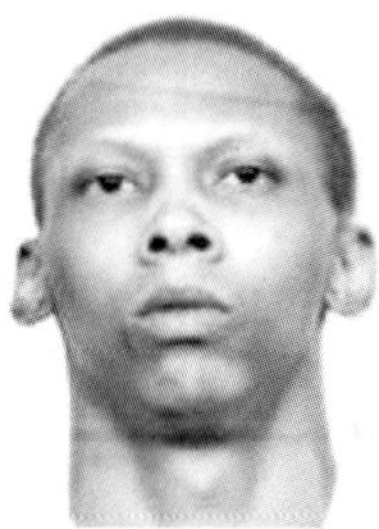

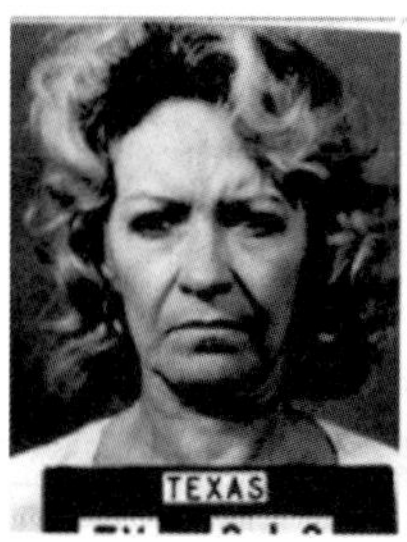
TEXAS

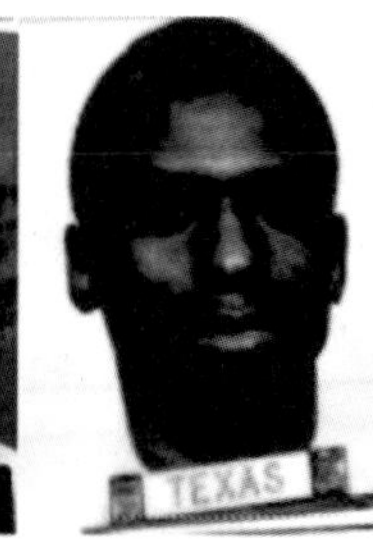
TEXAS

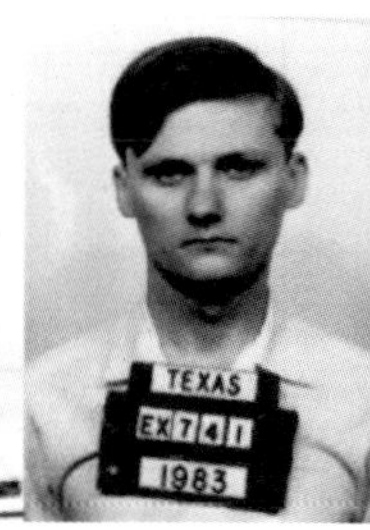
TEXAS
EX741
1983

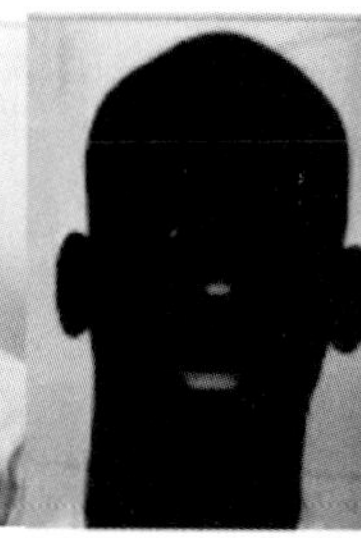

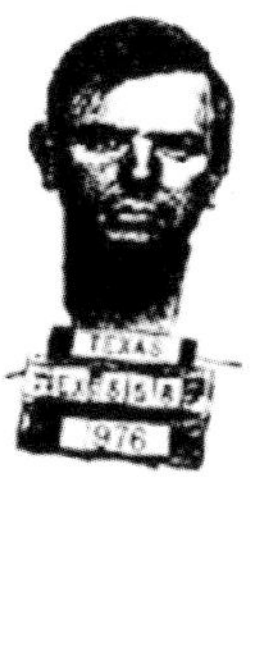
TEXAS
1976
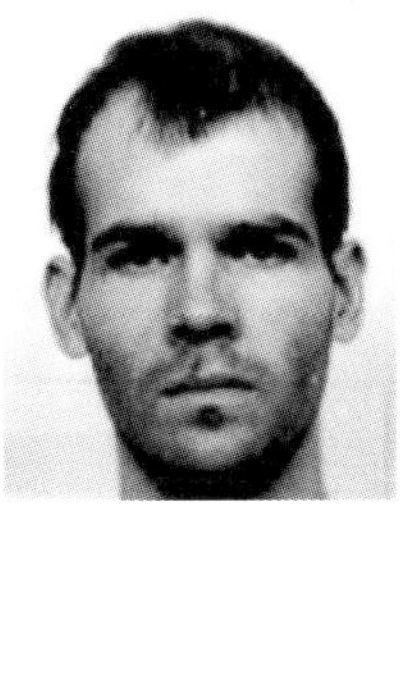
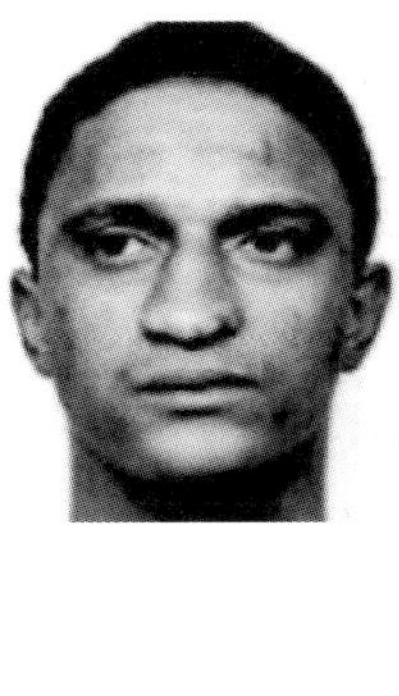
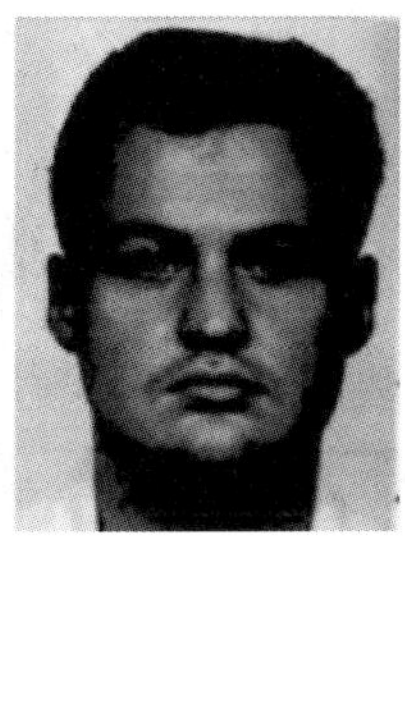
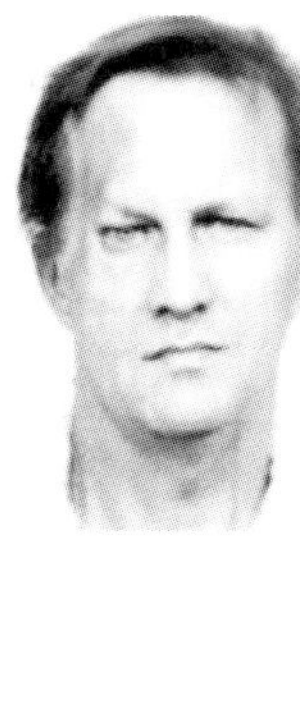
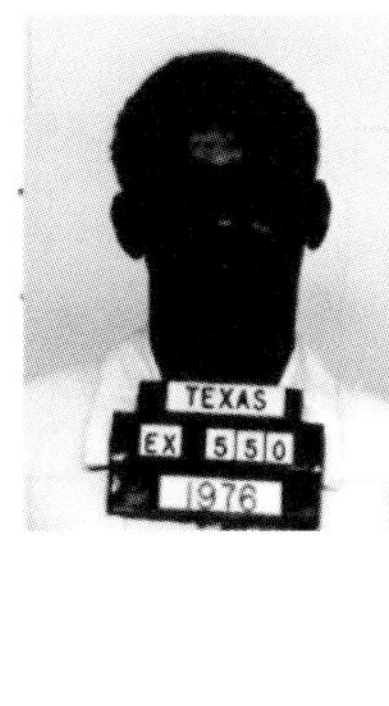
TEXAS
EX 550
1976

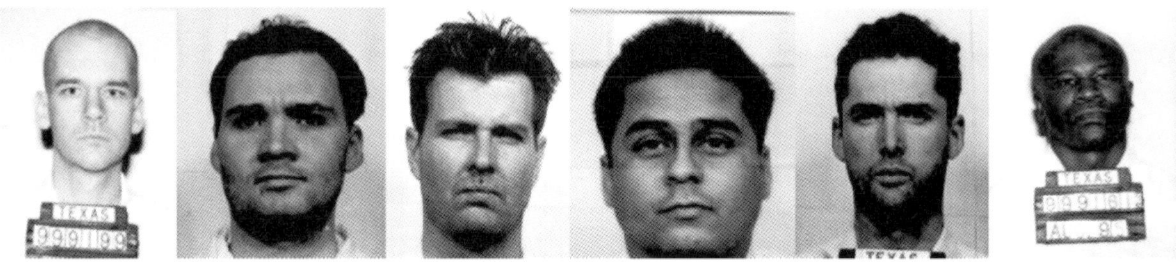
TEXAS
999199
TEXAS

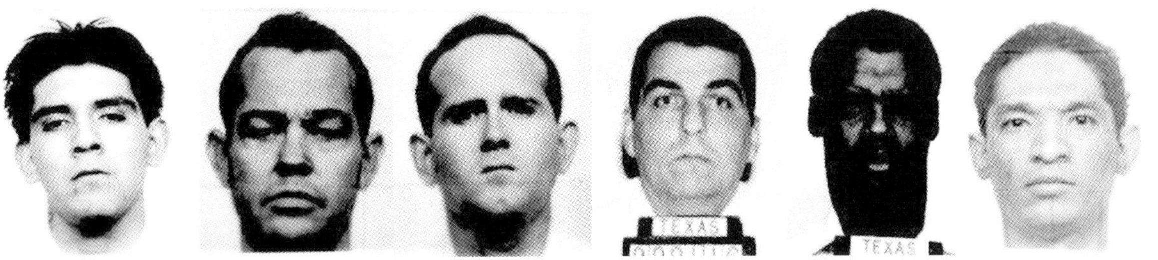
TEXAS
TEXAS

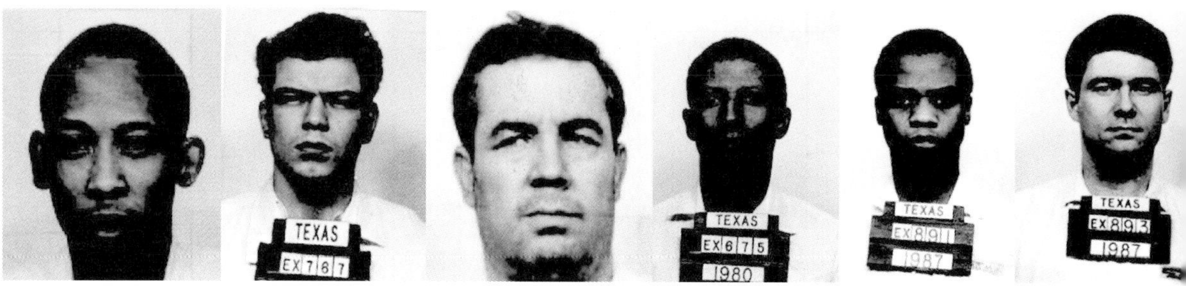
TEXAS
EX767
TEXAS
EX675
1980
TEXAS
EX891
1987
TEXAS
EX893
1987

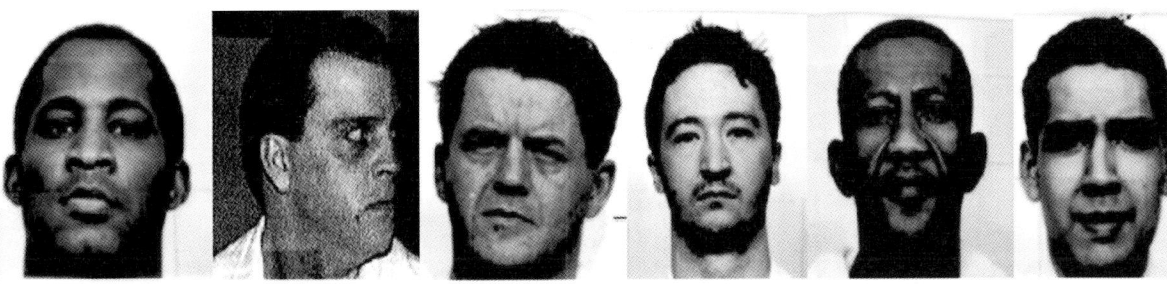

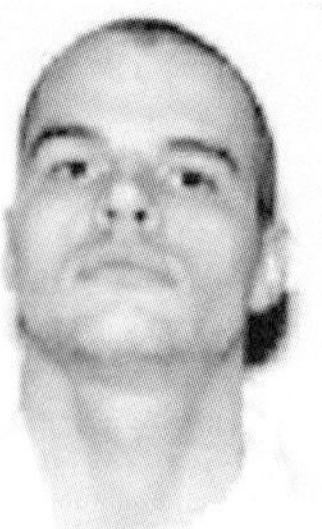
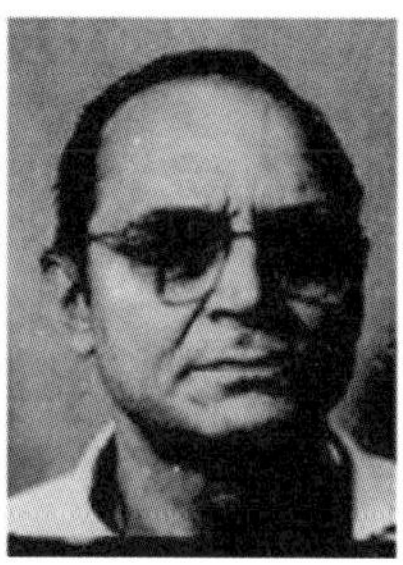
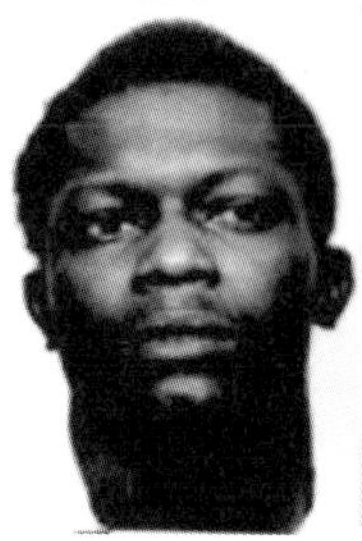
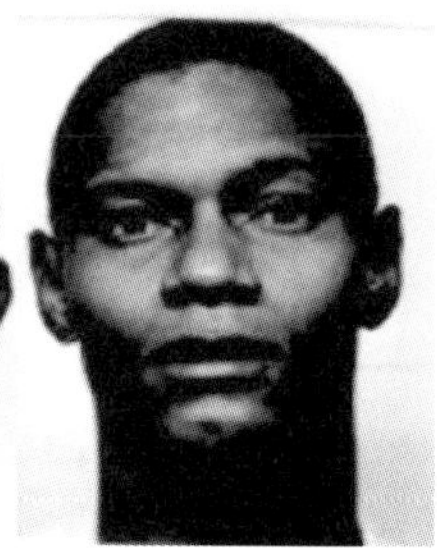
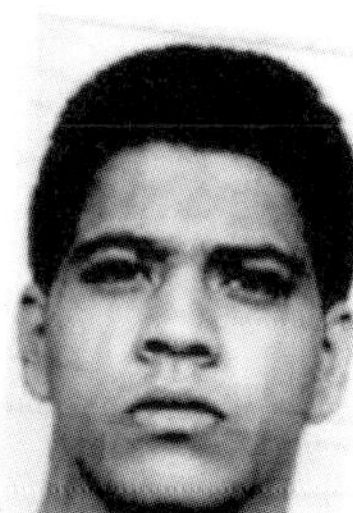
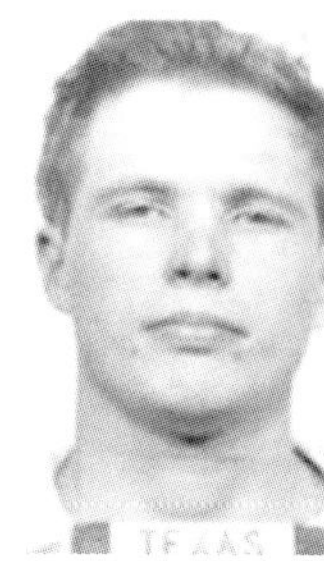

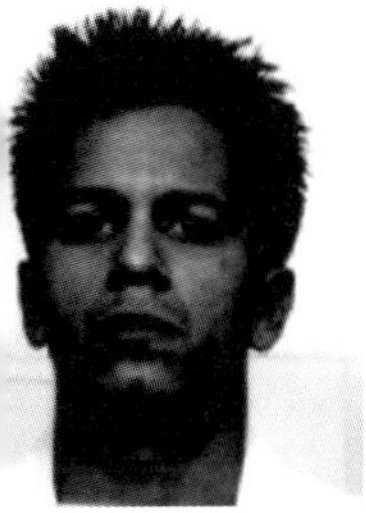
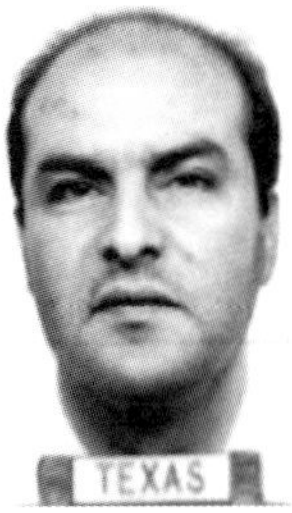
TEXAS
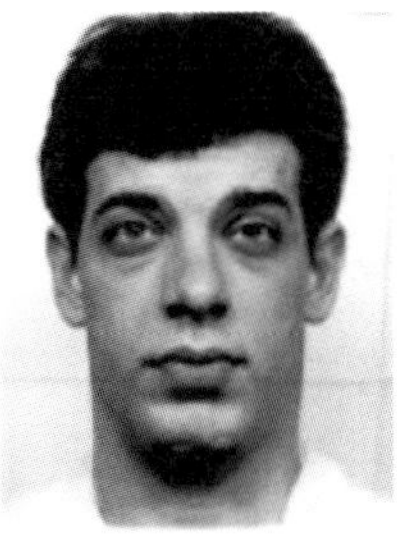
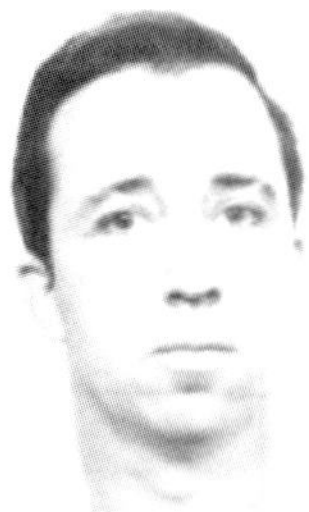
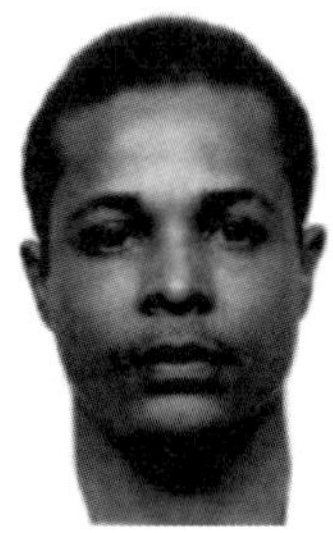
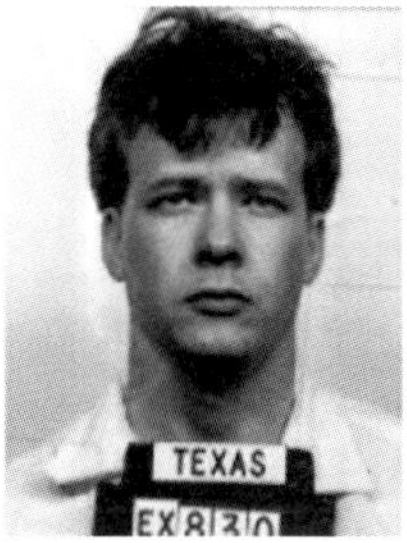
TEXAS

ZAGZIG SERIES

DIRECTED BY: PHILIPPE LANGLOIS & FRANK SMITH

IN THE SAME SERIES

LAURIE ANDERSON: *NOTHING IN MY POCKETS,* JONAS MEKAS: *TO PETRARCA*,
LEAH SINGER & LEE RANALDO: *WATER DAYS*, RYOJI IKEDA: *DATAPHONICS*,
GISELE VIENNE, DENNIS COOPER, PETER REHBERG: *JERK,*
CHLOE: *CHASSER CROISER,* SOUNDWALK COLLECTIVE: *MEDEA*
CHRISTIAN MARCLAY: *FIRE & WATER*, LORIS GREAUD: *CROSSFADING,* WINTER FAMILY*: NO WORLD*

1 CITÉ RIVERIN
75010 PARIS
WWW.DISVOIR.COM
ISBN 978-2-914563-77-2

IMAGES: MAUDE PLACE.
AUDIO CD ZAGZIG011 © VANESSA PLACE
THE SOUND PIECE «LAST WORDS» WAS RECORDED IN 2014
AT JAKE VIATOR STUDIO, LOS ANGELES, CALIFORNIA, USA;
FIRST EXHIBITED AS PART OF AV: NEW WORKS BY ANDREA FRASER, VANESSA PLACE.
MAK CENTER FOR ART AND ARCHITECTURE
LOS ANGELES, APRIL 9-JUNE 1, 2014.

PRINTED IN EUROPE BY
PETRO OFSETAS, LITHUANIA